BIGOTRY ON BROADWAY

An Anthology

Edited by Ishmael Reed
and Carla Blank

Baraka
Books

Montréal

ISBN 978-1-77186-256-1 pbk; 978-1-77186-257-8 epub; 978-1-77186-258-5 pdf

Cover design: Maison 1608
Book Design by Folio infographie
Editing and proofreading: Blossom Thom, Carla Blank, Robin Philpot

Contributor photos: Aimée Phan (Nicholas Lea Bruno); Carla Blank (Tennessee Reed); Nancy Mercado (Ricardo Muñoz)

Legal Deposit, 3rd quarter 2021
Bibliothèque et Archives nationales du Québec
Library and Archives Canada

Published by Baraka Books of Montreal

Trade Distribution & Returns

United States – Independent Publishers Group: IPGbook.com
Canada – UTP Distribution: UTPdistribution.com

For
Paule Marshall
Toni Morrison
Miguel Algarin
Rudy Anaya
Steve Cannon
Joe Overstreet
James Spady

Contents

Introduction

Ishmael Reed

Contributor Betsy Theobald Richards conveys the reaction that many of us have when cringing as we watch how others portray us in literature, film, television and theater. We lay out some serious money to be entertained, instead we are figuratively spat in the face by what's on the screen or stage, while others enjoy our discomfort. She is reacting to the musical, *Bloody Bloody Andrew Jackson*.

> I sat there, aghast, next to Mr. Eustis, my long-time Native theater ally and collaborator (we had worked together to produce two Native theater festivals and a few productions when he was Artistic Director of Trinity Rep and I was working for the Mashantucket Pequot Tribal Nation's museum). My heart was pounding, and my stomach turned, as I witnessed White actors in ridiculous redface, a humorous song about ten ways to kill Indians, and Native chiefs, such as the great Sauk tribal leader Black Hawk, falsely portrayed as turncoats and sell-outs. It was all met with uproarious laughter and applause from the rest of the audience.

Some critics were furious with me, my director, cast and even the Nuyorican Poets Café for mounting my play *The Haunting of Lin-Manuel Miranda*, which challenged the premise of the musical *Hamilton*, that Alexander Hamilton and the Schuyler sisters were "abolitionists." Our play, which cost us about $50,000, challenged the billion-dollar box office juggernaut, and was vindicated, according to Jeffrey St. Clair, editor of *CounterPunch,* when a research paper was released by the Schuyler Mansion State Historic Site in Albany, New York, entitled "As Odious and Immoral a Thing: Alexander Hamilton's Hidden History as an Enslaver." Written by Jessie Serfilippi, it concludes: "Not only did Alexander Hamilton enslave people, but his involvement in the institution of slavery was essential to his identity, both personally and professionally."

Our contributor Lonely Christopher provides the White supremacist background of the Disney Company, and how it was natural that it would align itself with a billion-dollar production that portrays enslavers as abolitionists.

Hamilton was heralded for being "revolutionary," but half a decade since its debut it feels like a historical artifact. It is specifically an Obama-era phenomenon, espousing watery neoliberal principles that were so attractive to the Democratic establishment that Miranda was performing his *Hamilton* songs at the White House before the Tonys. He was invited to Washington multiple times at executive behest and the Obama family and their high-ranking cohort returned the favor by making well-publicized appearances at the theater. Miranda was set up as a court composer for the administration, perpetuating a state-sanctioned prerogative for all citizens to ignore the unresolved legacy of slavery in favor of identifying with our national myths by venerating the Founding Fathers as "young, scrappy, and hungry" self-starters fighting against subjugation. Miranda's efforts in this regard were rewarded with a 2016 Pulitzer Prize and a contract with the Walt Disney Company. The underlying concept of *Hamilton* is that the sanitized version of U.S. origins is still worth telling, that the Founding Fathers can be idolized as long as there's a way to include People of Color in the pageantry. That's seriously out of step with the times, as more and more Americans are realizing that they have to actively reject the systemic violence that their society was built upon. The obsequious mythologizing on display in *Hamilton* is its greatest weakness.

The vituperative reaction from sections of the American intellectual elite to my play gave Carla Blank and me the incentive to examine what ethnic intellectuals and scholars think of how certain groups are portrayed on Broadway. Predictably, we found that their views are different from those held by the largely White male critics who can make or break a play. The plays that our contributors found offensive were praised by them. Their enthusiasm for these Broadway musicals, whose producers provided their publications with millions in advertising, helped sweeten the box office for plays that honored slave traders, Indian fighters, imperialists, and those who have perpetrated images of Black men that would shock D.W. Griffith and Julius Streicher.

Carla Blank is accurate when she enumerates the role that money plays in what gets staged on Broadway. Plays are workshopped and marketed to appeal to those who can afford tickets. When I interviewed some of the cast members and director of August Wilson's *Fences*, during a 1985 Yale production directed by Lloyd Richards, he referred to these audience members as "the plastic card crowd." One of the big money makers, which reaps profits to this day, is the portrayal of the Black male as a sexual predator. The efforts of Confederate novelists and film makers to exploit this type look innocent in comparison to the modern take on this product. I don't know whether Ralph Ellison, in his novel *Invisible Man*, had money in mind with his character Trueblood, an incest violator, but Ellison shows a fascination bordering on the psychotic which grips a wealthy White philanthropist when he is told Trueblood's story. The philanthropist is not alone. Novelist Diane Johnson wrote that "largely white audiences" are thrilled by the Black Predator Bogeyman type, and apparently, willing to lay out some significant money to be entertained by films, musicals and literature which promote such a character. Who knows whether Alice Walker had the cash register in mind when she created *The Color Purple* character Mister, who became the international symbol of misogyny and gave feminists from other ethnic groups permission to say what, prior to the film, staged versions of the novel would have been considered racist. But Walker did not have the power to place Mister in such a universally hated position. The late Toni Morrison said that it was Gloria Steinem who made the novel famous. It made Steven Spielberg millions more than what Ms. Walker received. Like "rock and roll," Black Womanism, however well intentioned, was co-opted. Both White men, filmmaker Spielberg and director John Doyle, one of those who staged a musical version of *The Color Purple*, expressed concern about Celie, the victim of the predatory Mr. Spielberg said that when he read the novel all he could think about was rescuing Celie. He put on his Indiana Jones cape. Neither Spielberg nor Doyle would have attracted investors to film and the stage to "rescue" women of their own ethnic groups.

What contributor Tommy Curry calls "the Black Predator," led to these women and men of other ethnic groups to climb on the "Rescue Celie" bandwagon without addressing how women are treated in their ethnic groups. Mister became all Black men, whether Black American, Caribbean or African, a trend that reaped huge profits for publishers and television and film script writers. Industries dominated by White males, who can write these scripts while sipping cocktails or snorting cocaine on the beach at Malibu. White men are not alone. Men from other ethnic groups also want to rescue Celie. A scholar who wrote a book about Richard Wright's misogyny hails from a culture where women who advocate for women drivers are jailed.

Another filmmaker of Indian ancestry, Pratibha Parmar, got a green light from PBS feminists to create a film, *Beauty in Truth*, that criticized both Black men and women for not enjoying the Steven Spielberg film. She is a member of a culture where women are subjected to honor killings and where thousands of women are slaves. So, after Gloria Steinem internationalized Mister, White feminist Marsha Norman got in some whacks at the Black male predator and made money too. She wrote the book for Broadway's 2005-2008 musical version of *The Color Purple*, collaborating with show doctor/ director John Doyle, which found her deferential to this White male patriarch. Judging from the lyrics by Brenda Russell, Allee Willis and Stephen Bray, which I have read, the musical combined *Cabin in The Sky* with *Green Pastures*. Not only did those outside of the Black experience make money from the film and musical versions of *The Color Purple,* but Tommy Curry reminds us that the Black predator has become a staple for Women's Studies Departments—Black Bogeyman Studies. Since there are few Black women faculty members present on the staffs of American colleges and universities, Black womanists are being short-changed there too. The late June Jordan said that she left Women's Studies because it was too dependent upon French patriarchal theory. For countering Black Bogeyman theory, powerful academic feminists made certain that Tommy Curry couldn't find work in the United States; he now teaches at the University of Edinburgh in Scotland.

Just as Alice Walker can't be held responsible for how White patriarchs and White feminists interpreted her novel, Charles Yu was not responsible for what interpreters made of his novel, *Flower Drum Song*. Though well received by ethnic audiences at the time, contributor Shawn Wong found *Flower Drum Song* racist. Contributor Aimee Phan discusses the stereotype-loaded musical *Ms. Saigon*. Both demonstrate that a lot of seductive bad dance numbers and show tunes can distract from a musical's text. In an interview, novelist and professor Shawn Wong said:

> At the time it was interesting because it was positive because there was not a portrayal like that anywhere on the silver screen before that. It was so stereotyped but at least we were being talented. We were singing and dancing and speaking English without an accent. It was completely racist, but at the same time I think a lot of Chinese Americans celebrated it.

Novelist and professor Aimee Phan writes:

> When I was fifteen, my family traveled to New York to visit my aunt, recently arrived from Vietnam. She was the last of my father's family to immigrate

to the US, finally doing so after multiple escape attempts after the end of the war. *Miss Saigon* was our family's first Broadway show, and we were excited. Since its London premiere in 1989, *Miss Saigon* experienced commercial worldwide success, with tours and revivals continuing today. It is Broadway's thirteenth longest running show. We'd never seen Vietnamese characters on stage before, and were hopeful, seeing how *Les Mis* glorified French rebels, casting them as complex and nuanced heroes. Perhaps this musical could offer the Vietnamese, so often stereotyped as peasants or prostitutes in Vietnam War films and television shows, the same opportunity?

We should have known better. The opening number, "The Heat Is on in Saigon," almost made us leave, startling my conservative parents with the revealing bikinis and thongs of the Vietnamese sex workers on stage, gyrating against the American marine officers. The show unfolded with the same tired stereotypes of the Vietnamese people as either hookers, victims or Communist devils. It also employed yellowface in the casting of The Engineer, a half-Vietnamese half-French entrepreneur bent on, once again, pimping out a young nubile Vietnamese heroine to an American soldier.

Contributor Yuri Kageyama, author of the classic poem, "Little Yellow Slut," also writes about the set roles accorded Asian American women, but she could be talking about Black, Puerto Rican American and Native American women as well. She writes:

The Japanese woman portrayed in Giacomo Puccini's early 1900s opera *Madame Butterfly* is that fetish supreme, a doll to be played with, then forgotten, a no-strings-attached consumable object of transient lust.

She waits and waits and waits, selfless, full of trust and forgiveness.

The White male isn't ever held accountable, except in reproachful looks and gasps of singsong horror.

The woman of color drinks in her oppression in a swooning soprano of submission.

In a fitting metaphor, she blindfolds her half-White son.

She kills herself, stabbing herself with the hara-kiri dagger of her father, symbolic of the dead-end pagan society of her ancestors.

To be fair, according to the script, Butterfly is only 15 when she meets her White prince on a white horse.

Contributor Emil Guillermo finds the same stock racist send-ups in *South Pacific*.

It has to be said that the sexist overtones of Post-World War II America are at times even more cringeworthy than the racist ones in *South Pacific*. While the White women are all 'dames' and objecti-fied as such, it's countered with the image of the strong conniving woman, 'Bloody Mary,' played with a menacing charm by the late actress, Juanita Hall, an African American in real life who could pass as a dark-skinned Polynesian. It's like a casting precursor to *Hamilton*, only here it's replacing a fringe 'other'—an obscure Pacific Islander—with a

Black who passes for Asian. (Is that Kosher?) Or is 'Asian' the gateway drug cure-all for all racism? A half-step or shade at a time? Curiously, other than Hall, I didn't see any Black faces in this anti-bigotry tale. Asian was just easier to handle in 1949.

From her intro set piece to her alluring 'Bali Hai,' Bloody Mary makes things happen in *South Pacific*. She's the charming grass-skirt dealer who sees pimping her young daughter to an officer as the best opportunity to better life for her family.

In sum, we have a grand confection of a musical, sprinkled with a bit of troubling bigotry, but nothing that challenges the realm of acceptable American racist behavior too much, not even in the '40s or '50s and certainly not now.

Some of the most offensive portrayals of colored ethnics on Broadway were created by members of ethnic groups that have been derided on stage, film and theater by others. A nineteenth century Irish American song and dance man, T.D. "Daddy" Rice, borrowed a little step created by Jim Crow, a physically disabled slave, which he called the "Jump Jim Crow" and it made Rice famous. Some of these composers and lyricists of musicals that colored ethnics found offensive were Jews who, alienated from their origins, directed the same stereotypes at Blacks that are still directed at their group.

Though they saw America as a melting pot, their part didn't melt. These composers and lyricists existed in an Identity No Man's Land, which might have contributed to Richard Rodger's psychiatric problems. They were not accepted by Whites and saw their route to Americanization by impersonating Blacks. Of course, Irving Berlin borrowed from the Irish and Poles as a part of his song repertoire. Why didn't that make him American? Why did donning Blackface make Irish Black imitator T.D. Rice more American? And if impersonating Blacks makes one American, then whom do Blacks, who still haven't been accepted as Americans, have to imitate to be considered Americans? Berlin, the composer of Coon Songs, did more than impersonate Blacks. He stole his first big hit, "Alexander's Ragtime Band," from Scott Joplin.

Contributor Jack Foley writes:

> Jewish Irving Berlin probably never experienced a Christmas like the one he describes in his song, but he might have dreamed of one or visited friends who were celebrating the holiday: not a 'Hanukkah Bush' but a tree that glistened with light. The I of the chorus is not the composer Irving Berlin: the I of the song is—in Delmore Schwartz's phrase—"a true blue American," a person who by definition does not carry the historical burden of being Jewish. The song is not only deeply about longing but about the possibility of assimilation as well. Many Jews were immensely successful in America, but they were not quite—white.

No group has been more maligned by Broadway, Hollywood and other forms of popular culture than Native Americans who will never be forgiven for their resistance to the invasion of America.

Drama critic and contributor Soraya McDonald writes:

> In 1838 and 1839, President Andrew Jackson forced thousands of Native Americans to abandon their homes east of the Mississippi. Even though Oklahoma was the end point of the genocidal forced migration known as the Trail of Tears, *Oklahoma!* doesn't feature a single Native American character. In fact, its only explicitly non-White character is Ali Hakim, a Persian peddler who seeks romantic encounters that don't come with marital strings.

Contributor David Yearsley, a music critic, writes:

> While White Supremacists were staging a Nuremberg-style Nazi torchlight parade down in Dixie last Friday night I joined an almost exclusively White audience on the verdant shores of Otsego Lake just north of Cooperstown, New York, at the Glimmerglass Opera House for a staged entertainment about American ethnic cleansing, one so effective in its procedures that all the ethnics had indeed been scrubbed from the story, if not from the cast. With its feast of winning songs and swirling dances crowned by a jury-tampering frontier-justice happy ending, Rodgers and Hammerstein's *Oklahoma!* is as American as apple pie and broken treaties.

Critiquing *The Book of Mormon*, contributor Claire J. Harris reminds us that the popular image of Africans, that of a people who boil other humans in cauldrons, persists.

I had no idea the story was even set in Uganda, or I probably would have thought twice before buying a ticket. Instead, I spent $100 to feel horrendously uncomfortable in a theatre full of White people laughing uproariously as one racist trope was rolled out after another. Although my urge was to leave at the interval, I went back in hoping the musical would somehow cleverly undermine the stereotypes it had set up.

The most self-aware moment is when the two White missionaries gleefully claim to be as African as Bono during a song called "I am Africa." They go on to list a complete range of African stereotypes: "Zulu spear," "running barefoot," "primitive," "endowed," etc. The problem is, the narrative does not critique these caricatures but serves only to reinforce them.

Finally, contributor Nancy Mercado writes:

In the end, after 60 years, Puerto Ricans are still not the ones telling their *West Side Story*. White American men continue to be the ones telling our story, defining who we are and ultimately, as the "superior race" and the dominant class, colonizing us all over again. In a feature for the *New York Times Magazine*, Sasha Weiss wondered whether this current generation of Latinx dancers 'will one day insist on staging *West Side Story* for themselves' (Del Valle Schorske).

She's right. When do we get to tell our story?

Foreword:
Is Broadway about
Dollars and Cents?

Carla Blank

In a 2019 interview with the Daily Beast, Tony Award-winning *Hadestown* star André de Shields explained, "The Great White Way is not called that for racial reasons, but because many years ago it was electrified and it appeared as if it were daylight all the time. But it's a marvelous metaphor if you want to discuss racism, because for so many generations we of color have been taught this is an inhospitable environment."[1]

To understand how completely inhospitable to diversity the Broadway environment has been and continues to be, one only has to examine the statistics of the business of Broadway: who produces the shows; who is hired to write the scripts and compose the music; who gets hired to perform as actors, singers, dancers, and musicians; who is hired to design, build and maintain the stage sets, costumes, lighting, hand props; who is hired to work backstage as the stage managers and tech crews, and who buys the tickets, etc. Luckily, because of increasing pressure within the industry in recent years, a few studies have been published that back up de Shields' assertion with unambiguous figures. In addition, they reveal that there have been other consistent Broadway biases that also extend throughout the rest of the American theater industry. These are the long-entrenched gender biases, against women and the LGBT+ community. And, like systemic discrimination patterns grounded in race and ethnicity, Broadway's patterns of discrimination based on gender or disabilities are revealed in both employment patterns and payment patterns.

Charlotte St. Martin, president of The Broadway League, the trade association of the Broadway theater industry, when interviewed about the state of Broadway in early 2020, said, "There are 97,000 jobs attached to Broadway for both the people we employ or cause to be employed."[2] Therefore, considering that in 2018, New York City's population was recorded at 8.399 million or that New York's metropolitan area was recorded to have a total population of 20.3 million in 2017, this industry makes a considerable contribution to the economic health of the region even though the home residence of any production's hires may be located outside of New York City. Just to give you some way to assess how Broadway's hiring practices align with the diversity of its hometown population, according to New York City's decimal census for 2010, the city's residents were recorded to be 26 percent Black, 13 percent Asian, 26 percent Hispanic, 33 percent White and 4.9 percent other.[3]*

No statistics were available for the 2019-2020 Broadway season, reflecting the fact that Broadway theaters have been closed since March 12, 2020, after Mayor Bill de Blasio declared a state of emergency due to the Covid-19 pandemic. As of Fall 2020, Broadway and Off-Broadway theaters are projected to remain closed at least through May 30, 2021. At the time of the emergency closure, Ms. St. Martin told Spectrum News that "31 productions were running, including eight new shows in previews. Eight additional productions were in rehearsals that were preparing to open this past spring. It'll be up to each individual show when they reopen after May 30, but according to sources, the long-running *The Phantom of the Opera* and *The Lion King* will most likely not reopen until the fall of 2021."[4]

---

* The U. S Census Bureau estimated that the U.S. population as of July 1, 2019 was 328,239,523. Their "Race and Hispanic Origin" count breaks down into the following percentages: White alone, 76.3%; Black or African American alone:13.4%; American Indian and Alaska Native alone: 1.3%; Asian alone; 5.9%; Native Hawaiian and other Pacific Islander alone: 0.2%; Two or more races: 2.8%; Hispanic or Latino: 18.5%; White alone, not Hispanic or Latino: 60.1%; Foreign born persons (2014-18): 13.5%. And the percentage of the population identifying as female was 50.8%. https://www.census.gov/quickfacts/fact/table/US/PST040219#PST040219

Therefore, this essay's discussion will be based on statistics gathered no later than the 2018-2019 season by various organizations in the industry, including two surveys from Actors' Equity, the powerful union for performers and stage managers, and two coalitions of theater artists of color. (The union that represents operatic, choral and dance artists is the American Guild of Musical Artists. No recent surveys of hiring or pay practices appear to have been made public by this union.)

Actors' Equity published a study of hiring biases in the Spring 2017 issue of *Equity News*, the first such study in their 104-year history. Across the board, their findings reveal that the Broadway industry has been more than slow to change its ways. Their statistics, reflecting seasons from 2013-2015, include data gathered not only from casts of new Broadway productions, but also from productions located Off-Broadway, in regional theaters and touring companies. They confirm that besides there being fewer work opportunities for women and members of color, they often draw lower salaries when they do find work. In summary there are "stark and pervasive barriers to employment in our industry for women and people of color—across all Equity contracts."[5]

Job categories covered by Actors' Equity are those of principal, chorus, and stage manager. In considering the following data, keep in mind that members of Actors' Equity worked an average of 17 weeks in the 2018-19 season, a figure which did not vary significantly over the previous four seasons. Of course, as in all averages, some union members worked far more weeks than the average and some probably didn't find work at all or worked for only a few weeks. Although stars generally receive salaries well above Equity's minimum requirements, imagine adding this limited window of employment opportunities to the other employment factors that many theater artists and technicians have learned to deal with year after year. Most routinely take jobs outside of the industry, such as teaching, when they cannot rely on earning a living wage in their chosen profession, or keep a side job with arrangeable hours to supplement their income, such as going the "classic" waiter or waitress route, working the midnight shift as a copy editor, or becoming a fitness trainer. It is a wonder how generations of people have continued to persevere in this industry, knowing these conditions, even including White male artists and technicians who, as the following statistics overwhelmingly show, are the most likely to be hired and most likely to receive higher pay. For example, the Actors' Equity Spring 2017 report stated:

> [...] we have learned that nationally over the course of 2013 to 2015, most principal contracts went to Caucasian members, accounting for 71 percent. Asian Americans: barely 2 percent. African Americans: 7.56 percent ... these numbers are

consistent with other contracts and opportunities offered to our members.

Equally troubling is the appearance of hiring bias when it comes to gender: Our membership is evenly divided between women and men. Consistently across all the on-stage contracts examined in this study, men were offered close to 60 percent of the on-stage contracts. For example, men were offered 61 percent of national principal contracts.

This study also shows that the problem goes beyond the stage and extends into the booth. The overwhelming majority (74 percent) of national stage management contracts went to Caucasians. In fact, stage management was the least ethnically diverse cohort in Equity's employment categories.

While women were more likely than men to receive stage manager contracts, they reported lower earnings. Women were employed on agreements with lower minimums, negotiated lower over scales and earned lower average contractual salaries than men.[6]

Another study, "The Visibility Report: Racial Representation on NYC Stages," from the Asian American Performers Action Coalition, extends these findings by their analysis of the 2017-18 season, in which they looked at 18 of the largest nonprofit theaters in addition to companies performing on Broadway in New York City.

Over 61% of all roles on New York City stages went to White actors, a rate double the population of White people in New York City (32.1% of residents). According to the study, 23.2% of roles went to Black actors, 6.9% to Asian American actors and 6.1% to Latino actors. That represents a slight improvement from the previous season, which had 67% White actors, 18.6% Black actors, 7.3% Asian actors and 5% Latino actors.

"Overall, nearly 80% of Broadway and off-Broadway shows' writers were white and 85.5% of directors during the 2017-18 season. Last year's report — on the 2016-17 season — found that 86.8% of all Broadway and off-Broadway shows were from white playwrights and 87.1% of all directors hired were white."[7]

The Asian American Performers Action Coalition's study also found that 95 percent of all plays and musicals were both written and directed by White artists during the 2016-2017 season. And as reported in *Playbill*, March 5, 2019, that season: "African-American playwrights were represented at 4.1 percent and MENA playwrights at 1.4 percent. According to the survey, the Broadway season featured no plays or musicals by Latinx, Asian-American, or American Indian/Native/First Nation playwrights, nor playwrights with disabilities."

The *Playbill* article reports that the Coalition's survey found that in their previous season's study, of all playwrights engaged in New York's 2016-17 season, 75.4 percent were male and 24.6 percent female. "Eighty-nine percent of playwrights produced on Broadway were male and 11 percent female. Female directors fared only slightly better than female play-wrights, representing 31.1 percent. Only 0.8 percent of directors included in the survey were non-binary."[8]

Another study, conducted in 2018 by Women of Color on Broadway, a non-profit organization advocating for African American, Asian American and Latinx women in theater, found "that between 2008 and 2015 people of color represented less than 25 percent of the theater industry. Last year, 196 individuals were hired as directors, writers, choreographers, and designers for more than 130 Broadway shows. Of that total, only 13 percent of directors, 24 percent of choreographers, and 13 percent of writers were women." [9]

There has been a little progress, according to the 2018 data collected in their first survey from 2011 to 2014, when "just over 3.4 percent of work being produced in American theater was by women of color; that figure almost doubled in the second surveying period, to 6.1 percent."

The Women of Color on Broadway's study also found that,

> the number of women of color who were classified as principals in plays, musicals, as members of the chorus, and as stage managers was dramatically lower than any other demographic.
>
> Caucasians made up a majority of all onstage contracts—principal in a play (65 percent of contracts), principal in a musical (66 percent of contracts), and chorus (57 percent of contracts). Caucasians

were generally hired with higher contractual salaries. African-American members reported salaries 10 percent lower than the average in principal in a play roles, for example.

Seventy-seven percent of stage manager contracts on the Broadway and production tours went to Caucasians. Over three years there were only six contracts given to African-American members.

"Of plays on Broadway, none were by women of color in the 1998-99 season," [playwright, screenwriter, founder and co-executive director of the Lillys, Julia] Jordan said. It was the same figure in the 2008-09 season, and in the 2018-19 season, of the eight shows by women on Broadway, two were by women of color; "representation within the underrepresented," as Jordan put it, adding that there had been zero female directors of color this season.

Jordan noted that the U.S. Census estimates that the country is made up of 20 percent women of color; the same figure went for those receiving B.A. degrees in literature, B.A. degrees in performing arts, and new dramatists at the Playwrights Center. "There's no shortage of women of color in the pipeline—until production," said Jordan.[10]

The summary that begins the *Actors' Equity 2018-2019 Theatrical Season Report* by Steven Di Paola shows that American theater, and especially Broadway, experienced a very healthy season, reflecting that the industry had at last recovered from the revenue drop which occurred during the economic recession of 2008, to even surpass earnings and employment of previous years.

The 2018-2019 theatrical season, which began in June 2018 and concluded in May 2019, was a highly successful one for the members of Actors' Equity Association. The number of Active Members continued to grow, a larger number of members worked than ever before, earning the highest amount of money on Equity contracts ever (within sight of a half-billion dollars), and members registered the largest number of work weeks ever. Some contracts, including the Production contract, which provides the financial foundation of the union, had their highest levels of employment since the recession that occurred at the end of the last decade. At the beginning of 2019, thousands of members mobilized for the first major job action in years that led to an agreement with Broadway producers that opened the door for Equity members who participate in the development of future successful Broadway shows to be financially recognized and compensated for their contributions.[11]

The increase in Actors Equity's total earnings reflected the increased number of members employed in 2018-19. However, as an Equity spokesperson noted, in non-Equity houses wage earnings are likely "more stark," as performers and stage managers do not have the advantage of Equity's representation and bargaining power.

At the conclusion of the 2018-19 season, Equity's active membership totaled almost 52,000, which was almost equally divided between females (49.99%) and males (49.81%) with the balance of the membership preferring either not to identify their gender or to self-describe, or to identify as either no gender or non-binary third gender.

Of course, statistics for the 2019-20 season, because theaters were closed in mid-March due to the Covoid-19 pandemic, will reveal a significant revenue drop across the board. As happened after the drop in earnings following the 2008 recession, the 2021-22 season is expected to reflect the beginning of a slow recovery also. Chris Heyward, executive vice president of NYC and Company, the destination marketing organization for the five boroughs, predicts that international tourism levels will not return to their pre-pandemic highs until 2025, although domestic tourism is likely to do so in three years.[12]

But Covid-19 related losses aside, why is Broadway so slow to reflect the diverse population of its home metropolis and the nation as well? The Broadway League provides clues to the economic dynamics often cited to justify Broadway's near exclusion of plays created by people of color besides the resistance to hiring Black, Latinx or Asian Americans to perform or work other jobs in Broadway productions. The statistics in their 2018-2019 demographic survey reveal that there has been hardly any change in the source of ticket buying income within the industry, as Caucasians have long constituted the majority of the ticket buying public. During the 2017-2018 season, the Broadway League reported that Whites comprised almost three quarters of Broadway audiences. "The average ticket buyer is a 44-year-old white woman, and almost 80% of all buyers are white."[13] Stated another way, women made up 68% of the Broadway audience in the 2018-19 season, which reached a record high admissions total of 14.8 million. Of those ticket sales, 3.8 million buyers were non-Caucasians and 2.8 were international tourists.[14]

The average admission paid for the following Broadway musicals, during the week ending 02/23/2020 was:[15]

Aladdin	$97.58 with audience capacity reaching		98.85%
Hadestown	$151.89	"	101.10%
Hamilton	$257.03	"	101.51%
The Book of Mormon	$122.71	"	100.82%
The Lion King	$140.55	"	96.54%
West Side Story	$104.47	"	100.00%

Of course, should someone want the best seats in the house, such as in the center of the orchestra section, those tickets will carry a considerably higher price tag than the average prices listed above.

These prices actually reflect the rise in ticket prices that has occurred since the 2013-14 season, when for the first time, the average cost of admission to a musical passed $100.00,[16] although again, the best seats had been going well above $100 for many years. So, unless someone is able to secure one of the limited number of discounted seats available through some theater's same-day lotteries or through such services as TKTS, it is clear that significant potential audiences are routinely excluded because of the cost. Broadway relies on New York's domestic and international tourists to comprise the majority of ticket buyers, as they are likely expecting to have to splurge on a Broadway show, because in fact, Broadway is one of the city's biggest attractions. But for many locals, attending a Broadway show remains a rare special event at best, especially when compared to the cost of seeing a film in a movie theater.

The biggest roadblocks to change are the high cost of producing a show on Broadway and the fact that most Broadway producers and theater owners are White men. Their tastes and knowledge are likely to exclude underwriting new works or revivals with subjects or styles with which they are not familiar or comfortable. Theater owners, such as the Shubert and Nederlander organizations and the Jujamcyn Theaters, who between them own 31 of Broadway's 41 theaters, can exercise the power to decide what shows they will house, what tickets will cost and when those shows can open and close.[17] Producers and theater owners want to invest in productions that promise market success, because they take a real risk. Just to develop a Broadway production, from scratch through rehearsals to the beginning of previews, cost upwards of $3-$6 million for a play and $8-$12 million for a musical in 2016, with costs increasing by the year.[18] Once a show opens, its weekly operating budget must be met by filling the seats. Again in 2016, the running expenses for all Broadway shows averaged $455,000 per week, with the most elaborate musicals likely to cost upwards of $750,000 per week.[19] These expenses include performers and technicians' salaries, theater operating expenses, equipment rentals, advertising, and royalty guarantees to the author, director, choreographer, designers, orchestrator, producer and co-producers, ahead of additional royalties due to investors, which may also be required to be paid out weekly.

According to the Broadway League, "only one in five Broadway shows breaks even, and those that do take an average of two years to show a profit…. Twenty-five years ago, it took an average of six months for a hit show to recoup its cost."[20] And because producers and theater owners control the money, their influence in choices of writers, directors, and performers can be huge.

That is why most Broadway shows are built around stars whose big-name recognition is most likely to attract audiences. In his article, "Why Broadway Is So White, Part I," *Forbes'* senior contributor Lee Seymour found that "Broadway's decision-makers simply don't prioritize racial equality. Several producers and ad execs—who asked not to be named for this piece—told me that 'green is the only color that matters ….'" Seymour concluded: "Another hurdle is our own innate bias as humans. We are predisposed to building communities around our own ethnicity, and as Broadway is mostly white, it builds on that. Again, some could argue this is racism. I would call it inertia. Producers and theater owners are not actively shunning minorities—they just don't see an incentive to reach out."[21]

Although not a new phenomenon, another example of that inertia, and a major contributor to the consistent lack of productions by playwrights of color is how many recent Broadway musicals are already familiar commodities rather than original works. *Kiss of the Spiderwoman*, *Hadestown*, *The Scottsboro Boys*, *Avenue Q*. and *Urinetown*, are among the few completely new shows that appeared on Broadway during the late 20th and early 21st centuries. Many productions are reworkings of films, like *The Color Purple*, *Billy Elliot*, *An American in Paris*, and *Kinky Boots*, and the Disney Theatrical Group's juggernaut of screen-to-Broadway productions of *The Lion King*, *Beauty and the Beast*, *Aladdin*, *Mary Poppins*, *Frozen*, *The Little Mermaid*, and *Newsies*.[22] This practice is sure to be continued, as of this writing, Disney is reported to have projects in various stages of pre-production development. Among those mentioned are *Hercules*, *Bedknobs and Broomsticks*, *The Princess Bride*, *Alice in Wonderland*, *The Jungle Book*, and

Father of the Bride.[23] Broadway producers' idea
of another sure bet is to revive classic plays and
musicals, such as the recent productions of the
musicals *Oklahoma!, Kiss Me Kate, Carousel, West
Side Story,* and *Porgy and Bess,* the George and Ira
Gershwin/Dubose and Dorothy Heyward "folk
opera." These revivals generally have involved more
diverse casts than appeared in the original productions, (except in the case of *Porgy and Bess,* whose
original all-Black cast refused to perform in front
of Whites-only audiences, causing some Southern
theaters to desegregate for the first time). When
significant changes are made to original plots, dia-
logues, and scores, these adaptations can be called
"revisals." Of course, changes to iconic works gen-
erate controversy. People will have opinions when
you tinker with a classic. Such was the case in
the adaptation of *Porgy and Bess,* renamed *The
Gershwins' Porgy and Bess,* which was produced
in agreement with the Heyward and Gershwin
estates. The revisions to the book were done by
African-American playwright Suzan-Lori Parks,
with musical adaptations by Deirdre Murray, who
is African American, and direction by Harvard's
American Repertory Theater based director Diane
Paulus, where the previews occurred in 2011. At
the start of the rehearsal process, Paulus, who is
not African American, explained her idea to the
cast, "that the original libretto would be fleshed
out—or 'mined,' as she says—to make the update

more like a piece of musical theatre, or a play, than an opera."[24] When transferred to Broadway, amid considerable controversy, it won a 2012 Tony award for Best Revival of a Musical. In an interview, Parks explained her process:

> So many of my ideas come from deepening the characters and their character's relationships, and deepen their truth in the plot, are really achieved by the music. The epic scope of the music, the beautiful recurring motifs, as I listened and listened, and relistened to the music I allowed it to inform the adaptation that I did with the book…. And this is where people get it wrong, not to make it "right, or make it politically correct."… Come on, gives us a break already. We wanted to make it better. Better… A more perfect union… (she sings joyously, as her voice trails off). Hello. Like amending the constitution, we want a better country. It's not politically correct… so the people get all the hair on the back of their neck up. It's not about that. It's about making it better. The music is Sooo great. Let us make the story just as great, if we possibly can.[25]

Racial and gender diversity has been slow in coming to Broadway, in spite of the revelations in studies by organizations such as those mentioned in this article—the Asian American Performers Action Coalition, Women of Color on Broadway, The Lillys, and Actors Equity—and besides the fact that in recent years, mass media outlets have been quick to call out the small number of awards bestowed upon people of color, women in general,

LGBT and disabled artists in all categories of the industry.

This status quo, justified by the need to appeal to majority White audiences who have been the defining market for Broadway's expensive tickets, has been combined with little outreach to develop audiences outside of the typically over 70 and White ticket buying crowd.[26] But now theater makers who are not White have organized, determined to change these traditional modes of doing business on Broadway.

In June 2020, following police killings of George Floyd, Breonna Taylor, Ahmaud Arbery, Daniel Prude and Rayshard Brooks, to list the most publicized cases involving African Americans who did not deserve to die that year, 300 theater-makers who are Black, Indigenous and People of Color (BIPOC) addressed an open letter to "Dear White American Theater." Signed as "The Ground We Stand On," it referenced playwright August Wilson's keynote address, "The Ground on Which I Stand," delivered at Princeton University on June 26, 1996, during a Theater Communications Group national conference. Immediately controversial with its advocacy for the need to develop exclusively Black American theaters and critics, Wilson said:

> We cannot share a single value system if that value system consists of the values of white Americans based on their European ancestors. We reject that as Cultural Imperialism. We need a value system that

includes our contributions as Africans in America. Our agendas are as valid as yours. We may disagree, we may forever be on opposite sides of aesthetics, but we can only share a value system that is inclusive of all Americans and recognizes their unique and valuable contributions.

The ground together: We must develop the ground together.[27]

In retaliation for Wilson's manifesto and the following series of exchanges in *American Theatre* magazine with Robert Brustein, then the *New Republic*'s theater critic and director of the American Repertory Theater at Harvard, Broadway's powers-that-be took a five-year break on producing another Wilson play, even though the Broadway production of Wilson's *Seven Guitars* had won the 1996 New York Drama Critics Circle Award for Best Play.

The June 9, 2020, "Dear White American Theater" letter begins:

We have come together as a community of Black, Indigenous, and People of Color (BIPOC) theatremakers… to let you know exactly what ground we stand on in the wake of our nation's civic unrest.

We see you. We have always seen you. We have watched you pretend not to see us.

And closes with:

And now you will see us….
This ends TODAY.
We are about to introduce you…to yourself.

The complete letter, which can be found in this book's Appendix, had 300 signatories including Cynthia Erivo, Viola Davis, Suzan-Lori Parks, Lynn Nottage, Lin-Manuel Miranda, Lauren Yee, Leslie Odom Jr., Lindsay Mendez, Leah C. Gardiner, Katori Hall, Eden Espinosa, Ruthie Ann Miles, Issa Rae, Jacob Padrón, and Liesl Tommy.[28]

In December 2020, June's "Dear White American Theater" letter was followed up by a 31-page manifesto by BIPOC theater makers, a work-in-progress list of demands for "accountability to anti-racism" in American theaters' hiring practices, working conditions, unions, and academic and professional training programs.[29]

There appears to have been some progress in the virtual world which became the go-to venue for many theater artists and organizations after the Covid-19 pandemic caused the shutdown of live performances. Perhaps this happened because of what we hope were embarrassing mass media disclosures of the surveys within the industry and the BIPOC theater makers' demands. Or perhaps it was because the internet offers anyone the possibility of bypassing the need for sponsorship by an established venue and can be less expensive than mounting a live theatrical production, pluses that many believe will continue to make the internet an important showcase for all after the pandemic subsides. We will have to wait for Broadway's curtains to go up again to know if any further, lasting significant changes will happen on their stages.

Great Moments with Mr. Hamilton

Lonely Christopher

Walt Disney, the racist, antisemitic union-buster, loved Abraham Lincoln. He adored the assassinated president so much that he created a robot facsimile of him, called an audio-animatronic. Disney made the automaton for a stage show at the 1964 New York World's Fair: *Great Moments with Mr. Lincoln*. Curious tourists would be herded into a room where a curtain rose, revealing the waxy likeness of President Lincoln sitting in a chair. His body began to move, as if he were alive. Miraculously, he stood up from the chair and began addressing the audience! He delivered an inspiring speech about how liberty is achieved through reverence for the law. His hydraulic motors whirred. "The Battle Hymn of the Republic" swelled as Lincoln took his seat again and the curtain closed.

This attraction was such a smash that Disney installed it in his new theme park the following year. He was obsessed with Americana and wanted to create a hermetic world through which to reanimate, for paying customers, his nostalgic childhood memories. Disneyland was a place where you could walk down the sanitized thoroughfare of "Main Street, USA," play "cowboys and Indians" on the wild frontier with Tom Sawyer and Davy Crockett, or sample a Monsanto-sponsored vision of the plasticized, modular future. There were no boxcars full of drunk hobos on the Disneyland railroad, no long-haired hippies riding *It's a Small World*, and the only People of Color around were Jim Crow caricatures, savage "redskins," or servile Uncle Toms.

The Walt Disney Company was founded on the culture of White supremacy. This is an inalterable fact. After the prejudiced patriarch died of lung cancer, his business continued to expand into new markets, becoming an international juggernaut. Strictly enforcing Disney's original sentimental chauvinism eventually started endangering the bottom line. But no matter how much the company reforms its image in the interest of sensitivity and inclusion, the House of Mouse is forever haunted by Walt's ghost: supremacy ideology. In the interest of heritage and continuity, the Disney Company has a bad habit of returning to its poisoned well for content. For instance, in the late '80s they built the log flume ride *Splash Mountain*, which was based on their deeply racist 1946 film *Song of the South*. (Three versions of the attraction were built; it was announced in 2020 that they would retheme the ride after the animated movie *The Princess and the Frog*.)

The American Pavilion at Florida's Epcot Center boasts *The American Adventure*, an animatronic stage show featuring Benjamin Franklin anachronistically chatting with Mark Twain atop the Statue of Liberty. This is not to be confused with the Liberty Square area of the neighboring Magic Kingdom park, which has a nearly identical theme. Liberty Square is modeled after colonial America, creating a glorified origin story for the national values that Walt Disney treasured. It's home to a haunted house as well as *The Hall of Presidents*, an elaboration of the Lincoln exhibit that features robot versions of every single U.S. president sharing the same stage. They have to add a new figure every four to eight years. After Donald Trump shocked the world by winning the presidency in 2016, *The Hall of Presidents* conspicuously went dark for an entire year. When it reopened it featured a canned speech from a grotesque new Trump animatronic, which to some looked as if it were hastily redressed from the likeness of Hillary Clinton. Robot Trump required his own security guard to make sure no disgruntled protestors molested him.

The Walt Disney Company is similar to a virus that hijacks healthy cells and turns them into factories to manufacture copies of itself. Starting in the '90s, this is what Disney has done to the form of the Broadway musical and the neighborhood of Times Square that hosts those theatrical entertainments. It began when Disney hired the team of lyricist Howard Ashman and composer Alan Menken to work on their animated features. Ashman and Menken had created the Off-Broadway favorite *Little Shop of Horrors* and kickstarted a paradigm shift by applying the Broadway musical formula to Disney's style of animation, resulting in the studio's Renaissance period with classic titles such as *The Little Mermaid*, *Beauty and the Beast*, and *Aladdin*.

This legacy was cut short when Ashman died of AIDS-related complications, but their achievements inspired the creation of Disney Theatrical Productions, which established a content pipeline from screen to stage. Soon Disney was opening shop in Times Square and mounting Broadway adaptations of their animated films. Most notably, they hired avant-garde director Julie Taymor to helm an adaptation of *The Lion King*, which has been running since 1997 and became a model for how Disney can assimilate diverse talents into its brand for the appearance of creative integrity.

Disney was a major force behind the effort to "revitalize" (that is, gentrify) the eclectic Times Square neighborhood, forcing sex workers and adult cinemas out of midtown Manhattan in the interest of providing a clean, family-friendly environment for their customers. Their theatrical division has produced over a dozen successful adaptations of animated and live action properties, many of which have played on Broadway. In 2020,

Disney's online streaming media platform released a filmed version (or *pro shot* in industry parlance) of *Hamilton*, the smash hit Broadway musical by Lin-Manuel Miranda about the life and legacy of Founding Father Alexander Hamilton that had been running for five years. Disney did not produce or invest in this project during its humble beginnings but scooped up the film rights after it became the hottest ticket in town. While they could not have created *Hamilton* on their own accord, the sugarcoated treatment of American history that the musical presents is perfectly in sync with the Disney ethos.

Before delving into the problems of *Hamilton*, it's worth taking a quick survey of how the Founding Fathers and American presidents have been used as subjects throughout the history of performing arts in the United States. Creators today dramatize the foibles and triumphs of their rulers for the same reasons Shakespeare wrote his history plays: to understand the machinations of power… and for the entertainment value, since world leaders get up to some spicy shit. Performance can also be used as a strong form of indoctrination. During the Revolutionary War, the Continental Congress banned theater as immoral, although plays such as the allegorical *Cato* by Joseph Addison were presented by order of General George Washington to encamped troops to lift their spirits. A common archetype of early American drama was the plain spoken "Yankee" everyman and plays such as 1787's *The Contrast* satirized Anglophilia.

Later, minstrel shows brutally mocked People of Color and enforced racial hierarchies. Abraham Lincoln was assassinated by popular actor John Wilkes Booth during a performance of the farce *Our American Cousin*. Patriotic skits were popular at the time, sending up current events, propagandizing, or heralding nationalism. As in morality plays, characters might embody simple ideas such as "honor" or "greed," or be portrayed as broad, racist stereotypes like "Sambo." Martin Scorsese's historical drama *Gangs of New York*, which is set in 1862, portrays a "Tom show" being presented in a rowdy hall (these were unauthorized, often derisive takeoffs on Harriet Beecher Stowe's novel *Uncle Tom's Cabin*). The figure of Abraham Lincoln hangs angelic from the rafters and admonishes "Dear little Topsy" to "cradle Uncle Tom's head" as he dies (both actors playing slaves in blackface). This enrages the spectators who throw rotting cabbage and tomatoes they brought for that purpose, screaming, "Down with the union!"

Such performance traditions flourished and evolved as vaudeville spread across the country through organized syndicates in the early 20th Century. Revues would include disconnected songs, scenes, routines, dances, and burlesques that often referenced contemporary political figures and social issues.

The modern "book" musical, with an overarching narrative, psychologically complex characters, and songs that are integrated into the story, is a more recent invention. *Dearest Enemy* is a 1925 operetta by Rodgers and Hart set during the Revolutionary War. It takes as its basis an incident where a colonist named Mary Lindley Murray distracted British soldiers who were chasing Washington's troops after the Battle of Brooklyn. She detained the British long enough with her hospitality that the American forces were able to regroup and counterattack. To a contemporary ear, the music is not that toe-tapping or remarkable. *Of Thee I Sing*, by Ira and George Gershwin, was a 1931 political comedy about a fictional presidential election, and the first musical to win a Pulitzer Prize. Rodgers and Hart were back in 1937 with *I'd Rather Be Right*, a Depression-era story featuring a singing and dancing Franklin D. Roosevelt. Years later, FDR would show up, this time in a wheelchair, to sing "the sun will come out tomorrow" with a plucky redheaded orphan in 1977's *Annie*.

Pop songwriter Sherman Edwards created the musical *1776*, which premiered on Broadway in 1969. It is set in Independence Hall during the debate over the writing and signing of the Declaration of Independence. John Adams is trapped in a stuffy room of fellow politicians who despise him, pushing for independence as part of a Congress that can't agree about whether or not to open a window. Notably it portrays the Founding Fathers in a candid, comical light instead of as infallible eminences. "You see we piddle, twiddle, and resolve/Not one damn thing do we solve," complains Adams. Sometimes the men break from squabbling to brag about themselves or flirt with their wives. In the end, only through clever maneuvering is a consensus reached.

The music is composed in a sometimes-catchy period style. Unlike the storytelling manner of Stephen Sondheim lyrics, these songs often dedicate five minutes to repeating a simple sentence or idea. *1776* makes an effort to address the problem of slavery with an out-of-nowhere digression where a South Carolina congressman sings "Molasses to Rum," a truly bizarre rant about how Northern merchants and bankers are really at fault for the slave trade. This is based on a populist tactic of the time employed to cast Southern slaveholders as honest and righteous salt-of-the-earth agrarian types compared to the hypocritical mercantile North with their suspicious and exploitative financial systems. Edward Rutledge belts, "Whose fortunes are made/In the Triangle Trade?/Hail slavery: the New England dream!" It's not a convincing stance. The greater point is that the Northern states came to oppose slavery while the South fiercely relied on it but since that conflict could not be solved within the debate for independence, the evil practice was left intact for nearly a hundred years (well past the abolition of the Atlantic slave trade) and would wound the country forever hence.

Elsewhere, "Cool, Cool, Considerate Men" is a number focused on the anti-independence faction of Congress who don't want to challenge the status quo that's made them wealthy. They sing, "Come ye cool cool conservative men/The likes of which may never be seen again/We have land, cash in hand/Self-command, future planned/Fortune flies, society survives/In neatly ordered lives with well-endowered wives." None other than the sneaky president Nixon pressured the producers to cut the song out of the film adaptation because he felt it was insulting to political conservatives. As of this writing, *1776* is scheduled for its hotly anticipated second Broadway revival in 2021, directed by and starring women and featuring Crystal Lucas-Perry, a Woman of Color, in the role of John Adams. It's hard to imagine this approach to casting wasn't inspired by *Hamilton*.

The 1976 musical *1600 Pennsylvania Avenue* featured a score by Leonard Bernstein and lyrics by Alan Jay Lerner and was a critical exploration of the first one-hundred years of the American presidency with a focus on the racist oppression of African Americans. The story interrogated the ruling class, asking who gets to be "American" and why, while juxtaposing the political intrigue of powerful White men with the lives of their Black slaves and servants. It castigated historical figures for their specific moral shortcomings and compromises that enabled a legacy of American racism. The show was sponsored by Coca-Cola and coincided with the country's bicentennial, so middlebrow audiences were outraged by its "unpatriotic" defiance. The failure was so profound that the show closed in a week, no cast album was recorded, and it was never revived. It is ostensibly a "lost" musical.

After Bernstein's death, his estate authorized a concert version of the songs, and that has been recorded and performed as *A White House Cantata*, although it too has had its share of controversy, lately being denounced as racist. The concert has at least once been cancelled due to a Black orchestra member protesting that its content is offensive. The progressive approach to the subject matter belies implicit bias and hegemonic smugness. The biggest problem with the lyrics is that Lerner chose to have his Black characters speak in a mimicked form of African American Vernacular English, which plays into disrespectful stereotyping and feels inauthentic. Lerner fixates on skin tone, creating an awkward sense of colorism equating Blackness with hue. This is evident in lines such as "why can't a darkie/hide out in da dark?" or "the future's looking bright!/bright and black/ that's a fack." The climax of the show also portrays the Republican GOP as a minstrel show, which is meant to be arch, although the idea of White artists toying with minstrelsy tropes is untenable even by the standards of the mid-70s. (It doesn't seem that the show used blackface and the cast did include Black actors in starring roles.) Despite its heavily tarnished reputation, this musical features some of the most gorgeous songs of Bernstein's vast career.

Contemporary American opera has often traded ancient myths for national ones, resulting in such important achievements as John Adams' *Nixon in China*. This 1987 opera, directed by Peter Sellers with a libretto by Alice Goodman, has become a classic for its sly yet poetic treatment of President Richard Nixon's 1972 visit to China and meeting with Chairman Mao. Although it has its campy moments, rather than relying on opera buffa caricature, the show presents a more nuanced consideration of world leaders without lionizing them. The result is a complex and melancholy commentary on America's role in geopolitics.

The composer Philip Glass has created two operas about the Civil War. He collaborated with avant-garde director Robert Wilson on *The Civil Wars: A Tree Is Best Measured When It Is Down*, originally intended as a performance for the 1984 Summer Olympics. As in their previous work, *Einstein on the Beach*, the themes are treated abstractly, but this opera included trippy arias from Robert E. Lee and Mary Todd Lincoln, and it was originally planned to include David Bowie dressed as Abraham Lincoln reciting the Gettysburg

Address in Japanese. Several decades later, Glass offered a more straightforward retelling of the end of the Civil War with his opera *Appomattox*. Abraham Lincoln returned once more, this time as a malfunctioning animatronic figure, in Glass' opera on the last days of Walt Disney, *The Perfect American*.

Stephen Sondheim's 1990 musical *Assassins* is about the disgruntled narcissism of those who bullied their way into history by shooting a president. The show takes the form of a revue where the murderers explain their philosophies and grudges in song. "Everybody's got the right to their dreams," a voice in their heads entices them, "come here and kill a president!" John Wilkes Booth thinks he's ending a tyrant's reign, Charles Guiteau offed Garfield to increase sales of his book, Leon Czolgosz was driven by militant anarchism, Giuseppe Zangara just wanted the pain to stop, and so on. Squeaky Fromme and John Hinkley sing a duet for their respective idols (Charles Manson and Jodie Foster) for whom they tried to kill Ford and Reagan. Other (sometimes attempted) assassins that have their say include Sara Jane Moore, Samuel Byck, and Lee Harvey Oswald. The show is a snazzy glance into the bleaker corners of the American dream.

Bloody Bloody Andrew Jackson preceded *Hamilton* by several years and is similar in concept, deciphering the titular 7th American president

through a contemporary cultural lens. Both musicals were developed at the Public Theater before
transferring to Broadway. That's about where the
similarities end. Alexander Hamilton has been
more of a neutral figure in the general imagination,
whereas Andrew Jackson is heavily reviled by many
for his genocidal populism. The genre chosen to
animate Jackson's life was emo music, which does
fit with the theme of whiny White male grievance,
although the result is entirely unpleasant. The
outright murderous criminality of Jackson is too
repulsive to cast him as a charming anti-hero. The
inept creators reached for dark satire but weren't
sharp enough to make it work. The book might as
well have been written by a jaded high schooler in
response to a sloppy history lesson. In terms of out-
rageously offensive comedy, *The Book of Mormon*
came along the following season and was a hit with
audiences.

Despite lyrics pretentiously referencing Sontag
and Foucault, the songs in *Bloody Bloody Andrew
Jackson* are crass and inconsiderate. For instance,
the number "Ten Little Indians" is just a snide
list of bad things that befell Native populations.
"Four little Indians hiding in a tree/One passed
out drunk and then there were three." With lines
like that, especially sung by an all-White cast, it's
no wonder several regional productions have been
cancelled after protests from Native American
organizations. While *Hamilton* has a superficially

affirming message about the American experiment, *Bloody Bloody Andrew Jackson* is sarcastic and irreverent. But its critique is ultimately nutritionless and immature. This musical thought it was living in the heroic period of irony, but it's just embarrassing. It was a commercial flop that lost millions of dollars. The director went on to refine his style in screen-to-stage adaptations of *Beetlejuice* and *Moulin Rouge!* while the composer died prematurely in 2017.

Lin-Manuel Miranda's *Hamilton*, based on a biography by Ron Chernow, is among the best musicals in Broadway history, while also extremely problematic. As a project that was first developed downtown at the Public Theater before moving on to mainstream success, it joins other shows such as *Fun Home*, *Hair*, and *A Chorus Line*. It was produced in a context that was overwhelmingly White. Even before it reached Broadway, most of the behind-the-scenes forces involved in its origin were White, including the orchestrator, set designer, sound designer, lighting designer, choreographer, director, producers, and of course Oskar Eustis, the artistic director of the Public. This disparity is the result of systemic racism in the theater industry. But *Hamilton* was the brainchild of Lin-Manuel Miranda, who wrote the book, lyrics, music, and starred in it, and who was already a major creative force following the success of his first Broadway show *In the Heights*, which told a story set within an uptown Latinx community. *Hamilton* is celebrated for opening up space in the consideration of American history and mythmaking for narratives that center People of Color. However, despite its blockbuster stature and undeniable luster, the musical fails to resonant with the contemporary social justice movement.

Hamilton is a musical about historicity, ambition, and consequences, but is most of all a love letter to its protagonist and an argument for his continued value and relevance. In the person of Alexander Hamilton, Lin-Manuel Miranda locates the spirit of oppressed people to rise up in society and will massive political changes into existence through sheer tenacity. From the outset, *Hamilton* assures its audience that it will prove how "a bastard, orphan, son of a whore" found it in himself to become "a hero and a scholar." An up-by-the-bootstraps narrative, to be sure, or "out of the ghetto." Hamilton is an Icarian striver, propelled from obscure and desultory origins to the forefront of a burgeoning nation.

He insinuates himself within the echelons of power, becoming a protégé of George Washington and marrying into a wealthy and connected family. When the U.S. achieves independence, he invents for the country ingenious systems of governance to promote economic prosperity. Many people resent his talent and want to destroy him. He foolishly gives them ammunition through rash decisions and carnal exploits. He encourages his eldest son to defend his father's honor in a duel, which sees the boy killed. Hamilton ruthlessly attacks his detractors in print when sensitive political conciliation would have been more expedient. But he is uncompromising to a fault, which is his undoing. He is slain in a duel with a frenemy who lacks his sense of ideological purity. Despite his flaws, the musical lauds the intensity of his genius and the fervor with which he strove to advance himself, his beliefs, and his country.

Hamilton was heralded for being "revolutionary," but half a decade since its debut it feels like a historical artifact. It is specifically an Obama-era phenomenon, espousing watery neoliberal principles that were so attractive to the Democratic establishment that Miranda was performing his Hamilton songs at the White House before the Tonys. He was invited to Washington multiple times at executive behest and the Obama family and their high-ranking cohort returned the favor by making well-publicized appearances at the theater. Miranda was set up as a court composer for the administration, perpetuating a state sanctioned prerogative for all citizens to ignore the unresolved legacy of slavery in favor of identifying with our national myths by venerating the Founding Fathers as "young, scrappy, and hungry" self-starters fighting against subjugation. Miranda's efforts in this regard were rewarded with a 2016 Pulitzer Prize and a contract with the Walt Disney Company. The underlying concept of *Hamilton* is that the sanitized version of U.S. origins is still worth telling, that the Founding Fathers can be idolized as long as there's a way to include People of Color in the pageantry. That's seriously out of step with the times, as more and more Americans are realizing that they have to actively reject the systemic violence that their society was built upon. The obsequious mythologizing on display in *Hamilton* is its greatest weakness.

In *Hamilton: The Revolution*, Jeremy McCarter makes the following revelation about the musical's casting: "[Ron Chernow] walked into a rehearsal studio in the Garment District and was, by his own admission, 'shocked' by what he saw. The men who were going to sing the roles of Washington, Hamilton, and the other Founding Fathers were black and Latino. Not being a rap listener, Ron hadn't given much thought to the fact that the people best able to perform the songs that Lin had been writing might look nothing like their historical counterparts."

The historian's impulsive horror at witnessing People of Color embody celebrated White men is revealing, but this anecdote explains something else important. Namely, that there was no ideological consideration for the conceit of casting People of Color as the Founding Fathers. It was a matter of choosing actors who were skilled rappers capable of performing the songs. Using contemporary, rather than period, musical styles was never defended as a conceptual subversion, either. Instead, it was pitched as a means of keeping the subject matter fresh and relevant, the same motivation a youth pastor might have for spitting a church rap for his congregants. *Hamilton* mostly shirks political critique, but it's easy to assume that the musical had invested in the powerful approach of "reclaiming" these historical figures that solidified American White supremacy by casting People of Color to play them. Apparently this was not intentional, despite interrogative reclamation being a major characteristic of the piece.

Chernow's portrayal of the Founding Fathers in his 2004 biography, especially Washington and Hamilton, is hagiographic. Using the luxuries of hindsight and confirmation bias, he damns everyone who was ever critical of Washington's and Hamilton's speech or actions as being preternaturally on the wrong side of history. America is great therefore it must have been founded by great men. Hamilton was the most driven, smartest, sexiest, shrewdest son-of-a-whore there ever was. Washington and Hamilton were heroically brave during the Revolution, painted as gods on horseback in Chernow's estimation, while their critics were simpering, anti-American fools. Never mind that following the Revolution, Hamilton careened from scandal to scandal for the rest of his life.

Miranda doesn't seem to have referenced any other sources, certainly not the research of Indigenous and Black scholars. He copies and reinforces Chernow's judgments wholesale. King George III, General Charles Lee, and Bishop Samuel Seabury are easy targets, but he also goes after John Adams with a vengeance, the "fat motherfucker" who needs to "sit down." That line is a reference to the song "Sit Down, John" from *1776*, which takes Adams as the hero of the Revolution. The 2008 HBO biographical miniseries *John Adams* provides a more even-handed version of Adams while casting Hamilton as a prissy, power-hungry edgelord.

Miranda's reliance on Chernow's work is obvious. Many of the musical's most distinct phrases and ideas are lifted directly from lines in the biography. This includes "diametrically opposed foes," "I am not throwing away my shot," and the Schuyler sisters' songs "Satisfied" and "Burn" (viz. "I'm erasing myself from the narrative."). Miranda mirrors Chernow implicitly in *Hamilton*, mostly unable to or uninterested in forming independent critical opinions on his characters' motives and values. Most exceptions are made for narrative convenience, like how in the musical Burr and Hamilton are relatively chummy until a major betrayal, whereas in the book they are painted as total nemeses for the start.

This overreliance on a single text is especially an issue because of Chernow's methods. His interpretations of primary documents are suspiciously selective. For instance, Hamilton's wartime letters to his buddies John Laurens and the Marquis de Lafayette were pronouncedly homoerotic, even for the florid style of the times. Chernow brushes that off, telling his readers that it's impossible to judge if these men were lovers. Much less ambiguous is the textual proof in Hamilton's paybooks that he owned and sold slaves. Chernow addresses this in a sentence, muttering that Hamilton "may" have been an occasional slaveholder, but moves on without even bothering to equivocate about it, or reconcile the evidence with his conception of Hamilton as an abolitionist. Chernow only concentrates on sources that support his arguments about Hamilton's sterling character. He sidesteps unsavory aspects of Hamilton's life through obfuscation and supposition, even going so far as to blame his wife for his infidelities by writing, "Eliza was either pregnant or consumed with child rearing throughout their marriage, which may have encouraged Hamilton's womanizing."

The Founding Fathers were human garbage, responsible for a plethora of atrocities. Land thief George Washington stole the teeth of the people he enslaved and put them in his own mouth. Thomas Jefferson raped his slaves and enslaved the children he had with them and forced his slave children to serve his "legitimate" children. John Adams made it illegal to criticize the government while deporting immigrants at will. John Hancock was a smuggler. Slaveholding Benjamin Franklin cheated on his wife prolifically and mysteriously buried a bunch of bodies in his basement. The pseudo-aristocratic duelist Alexander Hamilton was blackmailed (while running the Treasury Department) for an extramarital affair with a beleaguered woman. Aaron Burr, also a philanderer and slave owner, murdered a colleague while in office and was later tried for treason. Everybody was usually drunk out of their minds. They also fought and won a Revolution and established our nation and its government. It's obvious that politicians misbehaving criminally never went out of style. Even Barack Obama, neoliberal icon, was overly fond of drone bombing children. What good is it to suppress such details about these flawed national heroes?

It is an inconvenient truth, ignored by many historians, that Hamilton was heavily involved in the practice of slavery for his entire life. In 2020 the Schuyler Mansion State Historic Site published an essay by Jessie Serfilippi, titled "As Odious and Immoral a Thing: Alexander Hamilton's Hidden History as an Enslaver," which proved, through scrupulous attention to Hamilton's personal financial records, that not only did he facilitate the purchase of slaves for others, he personally owned them as well. Hamilton was attended to by a child slave (possibly named Ajax) while growing up in the Caribbean. His first job was at a trading post that bought and sold hundreds of slaves and he was directly involved in these matters. But the bulk of Hamilton's activities with slaves happened in the United States following the Revolution. Hamilton's own grandson, Allan McLane Hamilton, wrote, "It has been stated that Hamilton never owned a negro slave, but this is untrue. We find that in his books there are entries showing that he purchased them for himself and for others."

It is undeniable that Hamilton worked in the capacity of slave trader for friends and family during the late 18th century. It is often assumed that because he was a member of a manumission club (along with other unrepentant slave owners) that he was an abolitionist. Serfilippi argues that this was not the case and "not only did Alexander Hamilton enslave people, but his involvement in the institution of slavery was essential to his identity, both personally and professionally." She turns to primary sources to prove that Hamilton owned and rented slaves for his personal benefit, although the full scope of his slaveholding practice is not available on record. There is definitive evidence for the possession of several slaves, including one person that Hamilton purchased for his household shortly after he married Elizabeth Schuyler in 1780. Their daughter Angelica was later gifted a dedicated maid who was almost certainly an enslaved young woman, as Serfilippi points out. Hamilton purchased other slaves for himself in the final decade of his life, including a mother and her son (possibly named Dick). It is recorded that the child was rented out by Hamilton and that he died young.

Serfilippi writes, "While Hamilton was never noted as being attended by enslaved servants in public, this was likely because it was so common to see enslaved domestic servants in New York that it was unremarkable to people of his social class." So much for the portrait that Miranda paints of old New York being "the greatest city in the world." Slavery was so rampant as to become mere scenery. Miranda suggests a burgeoning, enlightened metropolis where there was mostly pig shit and bondage. It was a land of opportunity only for the ruling class of rich, land-and-people-owning, White men.

As a lawyer, Hamilton was hired to advise people in the purchase of slaves, such was his authority on the subject. He was a slaver to the last. After he was killed by Aaron Burr in 1804, his personal estate was recorded as including several (probably three or four) slaves. There is no indication they were ever manumitted. They probably either died in the custody of Elizabeth Hamilton or were sold by her to cover outstanding debts. Serfilippi concludes, "The truth revealed in Hamilton's cash books and letters must be acknowledged in order to honor the people he enslaved. Through understanding and accepting Hamilton's status as an enslaver, the stories of the people he enslaved can finally take their rightful place in history."

One might surmise that portraying a Founding Father without addressing slavery is like producing a musical about Jeffrey Dahmer that ignores his racist serial murders but shows him winning Employee of the Month at the chocolate factory. But proving that Hamilton was a slave owner does not invalidate Miranda's musical outright because *Hamilton* doesn't hinge on the mistaken concept of the man's virtues as an abolitionist. *Hamilton* uses as main characters several notorious slave owners while almost entirely overlooking the importance of slavery to the historical narrative. The musical cannot work unless the audience is able to feel sympathetic for slave owning politicians, which is no great dramatic feat as the entire mythos of the Founding Fathers relies on such cognitive dissonance. It's likely that Miranda would have gone ahead and made the same exact musical had he known Hamilton was a slave owner rather than an abolitionist, and the absence of slavery in his account would have been just as resounding.

Another disturbing omission from this chronicle is brought up by Melody Nicolette, who wrote that the musical "would have been the perfect venue to uplift Indigenous people." The action is set on Lenape ancestral land, but this is not acknowledged, despite being pertinent information to the story. Even if Miranda couldn't bring himself to wrestle with the implications of U.S. land theft and genocide, Nicolette points out that, "American colonists would have never won the American Revolution without the help of the Algonquin Nations being allied with the French." It's more "revisionist" to neglect this fact than include it. Alexander Hamilton is inventing the American dream as he is achieving it, but at whose expense? Miranda is once again taking his cues from Chernow, who overlooks Indigenous perspectives while claiming that Hamilton was a friend to Native people because a school he never visited was named after him, which educated the children of both Oneida Indians and White settlers. Meanwhile, Mark Meuwese writes that Hamilton "leveraged taxes [ensuring] that the American government had an army at its disposal that could be deployed to wage genocidal warfare against Indigenous nations." At best, *Hamilton* perpetuates the erasure of Indigenous populations from the popular historical narrative and, at worst, it conceals a Founding Father's complicity in acts of organized race extermination.

Hamilton's creators felt they had made their main character sufficiently flawed and multifaceted for the confines of the Broadway format. He is the hero of the story, after all. It's not as if including more historically accurate deficits or contradictions would satisfy the musical's audience. But Chernow's (and therefore, Miranda's) impression of Alexander Hamilton the man is so fawning and overblown that it begs contestation. Not all of Hamilton's ideas were instant classics. He lectured for six hours at the Constitutional Convention about his batshit plans for the type of government the fledgling country needed. It relied heavily on monarchist principles that saw many offices carrying lifetime appointments. Others argued against a single executive figurehead and the result was a giant compromise. Hamilton is often reduced to the venerated role of "inventor" of the federal government. Many of his ideas did prevail over those who favored state sovereignty and despised the idea of national taxation and infrastructure. The Federalist Papers, like the Constitution that it explains and defends, are revered by many, including fringe groups of originalists who believe that the meaning of these texts was locked down at their composition and should strictly apply, as written, to the present day.

Hamilton the musical blindly honors the first Secretary of the Treasury for making America. But it provides no insight into the complexities and problems of his economic policies, or the ways that they were architected to solely benefit White, male landowners at the grave expense of People of Color and all women. Even the Three-Fifths Compromise was a piece of legal maneuvering not intended to acknowledge the humanity of enslaved people but increase the voting power of Southern politicians.

Hamilton's work with taxation, banking, and credit was profound to be sure, but established a legacy of brutal inequity that the country still struggles with today. When the nation was figuring itself out, there were voices calling for the abolition of land owner-ship and private property, but they were handily defeated by cool, cool, considerate men with deeply vested interests in White supremacy and capitalism.

Hamilton embraced institutionalized perspec-tives on government and demonstrated a method for People of Color to exist within, rather than in opposition to, the established American mythos (despite it being, by design, racist and sexist). It endorsed the "better angels" theory of oppression, where all that is needed is systems of control to be opened up to a select few minority representa-tives, rather than demolished and rebuilt, in order to achieve racial justice. Because this kind of low stakes reform was the modus operandi of the exec-utive branch at the time, the musical was promoted by the powers that be. It is tremendously significant to see People of Color portray the Founding Fathers and for a Black man to become the president. But it also matters that the Founding Fathers treated Black people as property and President Obama made "collateral damage" of Middle Eastern chil-dren. Ignoring the unsavory details plays into the neoliberal obsession with optics over ethics.

Hamilton has been such a success with younger audiences that it developed a large online fan community prone to ridiculous scandals, including one where a teenage White girl forged an incredibly marginalized POC identity to bully her peers and commit wire fraud while writing fanfiction about Alexander Hamilton being a HIV+ high school student who falls in love and has condomless sex with John Laurens. (Her false identity was outed by the author of fanfic about Lin-Manuel Miranda being a cannibal mermaid). So there's that.

The message of *Hamilton* codified itself culturally through vapid fandom as well as educational outreach, with wealthy organizations like the Rockefeller Foundation subsidizing tickets for tens of thousands of young people. The musical is heavily fictionalized, yet promoted as a teaching aid in public schools. The Theater Development Fund sent scores of kids to *Hamilton* while enacting lesson plans like one that saw a White TDF staffer tell students from John Adams High School in Queens that Hamilton was "kind of a gangsta" before asking them to participate in a rap battle debating the "pro and con positions" of marriage equality (or the "tough issue" of "same-sex marriage," is what he actually said). Lin-Manuel Miranda and his investors will see their incomes bloat exponentially once the amateur license becomes available and schools can shell out for the rights to produce their own baby *Hamilton*, which in many unofficially segregated school districts will probably have a majority White cast.

None of this stops the show from being amazing, especially in the context of Broadway theater, which is a deeply conservative medium. The creative talent of the theater world might be liberal and overwhelmingly gay, but it's crusty old White male real estate magnates behind the scenes running the game. Broadway is controlled by two major syndicates that own most of the property: the Shubert Organization and the Nederlander Organization. Jujamcyn Theaters comes in a distant third and the Disney Theatrical Group actually only outright owns one theater despite their formidable presence. It costs millions and millions of dollars to finance a show. Investors want to back something that will have wide appeal, which explains the profusion of screen-to-stage adaptations that come preloaded with name recognition. Broadway shows are often spectacular, but even the great Stephen Sondheim was chased downtown in his late period for being a little too weird. The old razzle dazzle beats out quality and experimentation much of the time. This is about money. That's one of the reasons *Hamilton* is so special, because it's interesting. It's not just a hype machine. Every technical element is perfect. It's unequivocally well made, the polished product of industry-leading professionals working at full capacity. It's fast-paced, exciting, emotional, clever, and the original cast is indescribably great. The songs are catchy as hell. Miranda's lyrics might not stand up well to the best in hip-hop, but they hold their own against other contemporary musicals.

No wonder Disney wanted to get their hands on *Hamilton*. They didn't just want the show, they wanted Lin-Manuel Miranda. He could be their new Howard Ashman. Miranda has contributed songs to the animated feature *Moana* as well as the *Star Wars* franchise and appeared in the show *Duck Tales* and the film *Mary Poppins Returns*. Next up he will be writing new songs for the live action remake of *The Little Mermaid*, which was the project that launched Ashman's brief but lucrative career at Disney. He also has another original Disney musical in the pipeline. Uncle Walt has his hand firmly up Lin-Manuel Miranda's ass. Unless his goal was always to end up doing children's entertainment, it looks like Miranda is going where the money is.

In early 2020, Disney announced it had purchased the distribution rights to the original cast pro shot of *Hamilton* for seventy-five million dollars. A theatrical release was planned, until the Covid-19 pandemic disrupted the industry and closed cinemas. Disney was compelled to move several of their upcoming theatrical assets to their new streaming platform, including *Hamilton*, which premiered online in time for Independence Day. The film version of the musical was presented as staged, except for the censorship of the word "fuck" in two instances, which is disappointing because

Disney certainly has the clout to support Miranda's uncompromised script, but they chose not to in the interest of receiving a PG-13 rating from the MPA instead of accepting an R or releasing it unrated.

While *Hamilton* was the product of Obama-era neoliberalism, Disney released the film to a world turned upside-down. The vision of color-blind meritocracy that the Democrats weakly championed had been violently rejected in 2016 by Trumpism, a completely unstable political accident based on fear and greed. The inept animus of Donald Trump legitimized White nationalism and capitalistic exploitation. Hate groups entered the mainstream. The GOP was hellbent on undoing the accomplishments of President Obama, attacking the healthcare system in the name of private industry and the rights of women and queer people under the guise of "religious freedom." The Trump administration started out with a "Muslim ban" and family separation policies that saw migrant children stolen from their families and locked in cages. In the final year of Trump's term, a plague had swept the country that was being grossly exacerbated by federal inaction and mismanagement.

The Republicans had a remarkably laissez-faire attitude in response to an enormous public health crisis that battered the economy and resulted in hundreds of thousands of deaths. Lockdowns in metropolitan areas led to substantial job loss, which began to foment revolutionary sentiment. In a way, the pandemic became an incubator for social justice organizing. The Black Lives Matter movement, which had originated years prior, finally struck a national chord. A period of reckoning had begun. People of Color were forging their own leadership paths, not glorifying ancient abusers. Mutual aid networks were established through which people could help each other directly when the government refused to intervene. There were massive, widespread, ongoing street protests. People, organizations, and businesses were called to account for their complicity in systemic racism and sexism. Major companies scrambled to change their messaging to support People of Color. This watershed moment, perhaps comparable to the height of the Civil Rights movement, provided the sociopolitical context into which *Hamilton* received its wide release. Previously it was a more rarefied experience, one which people had to shell out thousands of dollars to witness in person at Manhattan's Richard Rodgers Theater (or catch the travelling production in the hyper-gentrified tech hub of San Francisco). That limited its audience to the wealthy. Suddenly the show was available to stream for the price of a Happy Meal.

Thus emerged a more nuanced and critical response to Lin-Manuel Miranda's treatment of the Founding Fathers. Actor/director Gabriel Montoya was quoted as saying, "Slavers shouldn't get a musical that ignores that they were slavers," adding that eliding the negative aspects of their lives is "covering over their crimes." He asked, "If we need to dress up as slavers, land thieves, and murderers of Natives to be seen as leaders, what does that say about us as a culture?" In light of such political discord and the expression of so much pain, it starts to feel as if *Hamilton* relies on a sense of national reconciliation and healing that simply never happened. Activist and teacher Ajamu Baraka tweeted that the musical "is racist buffoonery & revisionist history meant to make liberal White folks feel good about their collaboration with the colonial project [known] as the U.S. & its racist imperialist project abroad." The musical was also criticized for its diminishment of women, who have far fewer songs than the men in the cast and are viewed exclusively through their romantic relationships with the protagonist. However, *Hamilton*'s detractors remain in the minority and are casually brushed off as participants in mindlessly vindictive "cancel culture."

In *Hamilton*, Lin-Manuel Miranda carves out a place for Latinx and African American artists to identify with White (supremacist) folklore. But is the United States getting to a point where its early history and foundational myths are better rejected than celebrated? The musical is palatable because it's ultimately non-confrontational. Weirdly, Miranda cut a song about Washington's Cabinet debating slavery because it "didn't shed new light on the characters." Another fundamental mistake is how he conflated colonists with immigrants. He bought into Chernow's brazen assertion that "no immigrant in American history has ever made a larger contribution than Alexander Hamilton." By insisting that Hamilton's path (as a British subject) from the Caribbean to North America directly relates to the contemporary immigrant experience, Miranda erases the violent impact of British colonialism on the world. As Ishmael Reed wrote, "Hamilton was part of the Occupation by Northern Europeans whether it was in North America or the Caribbean." His journey from one British colony to another was more an act of White flight than immigration in the current sense.

Miranda's lack of nuance isn't surprising coming from somebody who as a college student reportedly starred in a Holocaust-themed production of *Jesus Christ Superstar* and went on *Saturday Night Live* to sing that Trump would "never be president" a month before he was elected president. In a post-Obama political climate, *Hamilton* may be commended for supporting a diverse cast, but its message doesn't read as truly progressive. Which is not to say that Broadway isn't capable of promoting intellectually rigorous work from People of Color. The truncated 2019-20 season included *The Inheritance*, a two-part AIDS play by Matthew Lopez; *Slave Play*, a scathing look at the emotional dynamics of interracial relationships by Black dramatist Jeremey O. Harris; and the Broadway debut of Charles Fuller's 1982 Pulitzer Prize winner about racism in the armed forces, *A Soldier's Play*. As always, the most daring work is to be found Off-Broadway, like Donja R. Love's *One in Two*, about HIV in the Black community. Directly after *Hamilton* hit streaming, Miranda responded to the controversy with a brief mea culpa, insisting that he did his best but, "It's all fair game."

Making Mister: Anti-Black Misandry in Alice Walker's Portrayal of Black Men in *The Color Purple*

Tommy J. Curry

In 1982, Alice Walker penned *The Color Purple*. This Pulitzer Prize winning text was made into a movie by Stephen Spielberg in 1985. An original Broadway production, with book by Marsha Norman, ran from 2006-2008, winning multiple Tony awards. Its Broadway revival ran from 2015-2017, winning two Tony awards in 2016, including Best Revival for a Musical. *The Color Purple* has not only been embraced as a literary work, but a cultural and conceptual representation of Black women's experience as oppressed and silenced (Cheung 1988). Much has been written about Alice Walker's *The Color Purple* as a liberating rhetorical and literary representation of Black women's voice. The depiction of Black men as abusers and rapists within the un-silencing of Black female voice became justified, a necessary means to an end. Over the last several decades, numerous academic articles and cinematic commentaries have justified the caricatures of Black men defined by Celie's father and Mister as conceptually grounding Black feminist theory and being an accurate depiction of Black women's experiences of sexual violence at the hands of Black men generally (Cutter 2000; Hamilton 1988). The discussion of Black women's victimization at the hands of Black men, while viewed as controversial in the 1980s, became a hallmark of Black literary traditions and contemporary Black gender theory. Mister has become a well-established trope of Black masculinity which defined not only the propensity Black males have for violence against Black women, but the Black male personality. Any criticism of this depiction of Black men was understood as anti-woman and a form of silencing (Lemons 1997).

Previous literature has assumed that the depictions of Black men as violent rapists reflected the actual sociological condition and historical circumstances of sexual violence in the Black community. These authors assert that the reactions Black men and women had to Walker's text were a continuation of the debates ignited between Black men and women with the publication of Michelle Wallace's *Black Macho and the Myth of the Superwoman* (1980) or Ntozake Shange's *For Colored Girls* (1975). In many ways, previous commentaries on *The Color Purple* began with the presumption that Alice Walker's text expressed the discontents of Black women towards issues of gender inequality and racial oppression that accurately described Black men. The growing attention to issues of domestic abuse and rape in the Black community gave these ideas the appearance of legitimacy throughout the U.S. academy and among cultural critics.

This essay argues that the previous debates surrounding the depiction of Black men in Alice Walker's *The Color Purple* have overlooked how the caricatures of Black men as rapists and abusers reflect the consensus of racist White criminological and feminist literature in the 1970s rather than the sociological reality of Black people across the United States. The racist myths used to describe poor Black men by Black feminist theorists and cultural critics were not based in any clearly established trend of rape and intimate partner violence being exclusive perpetrated by Black men but were instead the reflection of various debates and literatures produced by White feminists and criminologists to justify the incarceration and elimination of Black men and boys from American society (Stewart & Scott 1978).

The Color Purple

Walker's novel begins with the rape of Celie by her presumed father. The reader is shocked by the brutality and callousness of the act. The reader is held captive by Walker's description of Celie's father as he was raping her. "You better not never tell nobody but God. It'd kill your mammy," he says. Walker begins *The Color Purple* with the most brutal incestuous violence imaginable. Celie says her father "never had a kine word to say to me. Just say 'You gonna do what your mammy wouldn't.'" Celie then describes her rape by her father where he "put his thing up gainst my hip and sort of wiggle it around. Then he grab hold my titties. Then he push his thing inside my pussy" (Walker 1982, 1). This was painful for Celie. She says "When that hurt, I cry. He start to choke me, saying 'You better shut up and git used to it'" (2). On the first page the reader is conditioned to believe that the relationship that Black men have to their daughters is emotionally distant, physically abusive, and sexually predatory. It is impressed upon the reader that the Black home, or more so the Black family, is devoid of love and is driven by more primal sexual urges and violence. Celie's father prepares the audience for the horror of Black masculinity. There is nothing more sacred than the love of a parent for a child, but in the very first scene Walker strips the audience of this belief.

The audience witnesses the negotiation of Celie's father—a rapist—and Mister. Mister wants to marry Celie's sister Nettie, but Celie's father says that Nettie is too young and can get more schooling (8). Celie on the other hand could not have any more children, so Mister could "do everything just like you want to and she ain't gonna make you feed it or clothe it" (9). Mister and Celie's father believed Celie was ugly, but a good worker (9-10). They are depicted as overseers of Black women. Tyrants who used Black women's bodies for sex and childcare without concern for Celie's care or pleasure. This is depicted by Mister's oldest son throwing a rock at Celie that "laid her head open" (14). Mister was an abuser who taught his son Harpo to abuse women (23). This is made plain in Mister's exchange with Harpo's wife Sofia. Harpo wanted to know "what to do to make Sofia mind" (37). Mister asked Harpo, "You ever hit her" (37)? Harpo said no, so Mister asked "Well how you expect to make her mind? Wives is like children. You have to let 'em know who got the upper hand. Nothing can do that better than a good sound beating" (37).

Walker comforts the audience in their repulsion for Black men. Celie's father, Mister, Mister's father, and Harpo used neglect, sex, and physical violence to discipline women throughout the novel. The audience buys into the idea that Mister is not redeemable. Celie describes sex with Mister as if he is using the toilet on her (81). Throughout *The Color Purple*, Black men are depicted as having a generational culture of abuse and sexual violence against Black women. They teach each other how to hurt women by exploiting their bodies and commodifying their care of children and others.

The Origins of Black Male as Rapist Theory

There have been several very public commentaries concerning the role and accusations waged by Black feminist thought: Barbara Smith's (1983) scathing critique of bell hooks, *The Black Scholar* May/June 1979 special issue dedicated to Michelle Wallace's *Black Macho*, and of course the infamous exchange between Alice Walker (1993) and Elaine Brown (1993) in *The New York Times*. These debates centered on how Black people understood the stereotypes and narratives being displayed in books, media, and cinema. However, there has been very little consideration of the relationship the images of Black men as violent rapist had to mainstream criminological and feminist theories in the 1970s.

With the popularization of subculture of violence theory, there was widespread acceptance that Black people were more violent and prone to commit lethal violence than Whites. Black homes were thought to be violent places where Black men and women fought for domination over one another—often resulting in the killing of Black men by their spouses (Wolfgang & Ferracuti 1967). By the early 1970s, subculture of violence theory had developed into an explanatory account of not only the disproportionate rates of homicide within Black communities, but also of rape. Menachem Amir's *Patterns of Forcible Rape* (1971) became the hallmark of feminist theory. It allowed White feminists such as Susan Brownmiller (1975) to describe Black masculinity as culturally violent and prone to rape as a compensatory behavior for the effects of racism. Amir's work, which argued that rape was predominately an intraracial rather than interracial action, resonated with White feminists who saw currency in criminology's new discovery (Griffin 1971). By the mid-1970s, Black men had come to be understood as a contracultural type. The work of the criminologist Lynn A. Curtis (1975) argued that rape was endemic to Black masculinity—and that it was part of the cultural inclinations of Black males to abuse and sexually assault Black women for the slightest offence (70-71).

In the early 1980s, White feminists developed a theory of Black masculinity that argued "the male sex organ became the identity of the Black male as well as his tenuous link with life itself, for while he might be given approval for uninhibited sexual activity with Black women, the least suggestion of sexual behavior with White women was to invite castration and/or death" (Holmes & Williams 1981, 31). The sexually violent Black male was not the result of an earnest study of the Black male, but decades of criminological and feminist theory designed to castigate Black men and boys.

Conclusion

The idea of Black males fighting for civil rights and Black Power was not the product of Black women's experience as much as it was the extension of White criminological and White feminist theory describing Black masculinity (Firestone 1970). The gender debates happening among Black academics and cultural critics did not simply reflect the intra-racial dissent over the nature of sexism, patriarchy, and masculinity in the Black community. These debates also reflected the extent to which previously established theories about Black men and boys paralleled the cinematic depictions of Black males broadcast to the world under the guise of female empowerment. The Black rapist and abuser became not only the lynchpin for gender theories proposed by feminists, but a mainstay of Black literary theory and scholarship.

Works Cited

Amir, Menachem. 1971. *Patterns in Forcible Rape*. Chicago: University of Chicago Press.

Bobo, Jacqueline. 1988. "Black Women's Responses to The Color Purple." *Jump Cut: A Review of Contemporary Media* 33: 43-51.

Brown, Elaine. 1993. "Attack Racism, Not Black Men." *The New York Times*, May 25: A23.

Brownmiller, Susan. 1975. *Against Our Will: Men, Women, and Rape*. New York: Fawcett Columbine.

Cheung, King-Kok. 1988. "Imposed Silences in The Color Purple and The Woman Warrior." *PMLA* 103 (2): 162-174.

Curtis, Lynn A. 1975. *Violence, Race, and Culture.* Lexington, MA: Lexington Books.

Cutter, Martha J. 2000. "Philomela Speaks: Alice Walker's Revisioning of Rape Archetypes in The Color Purple." *MELUS* 25 (3-4): 161-180.

Editor. 1985. "How to Close the Widening and Dangerous Gap between Black Men and Women." *Ebony* 40 (4): 60-66.

Firestone, Shulamith. 1970. *The Dialectic of Sex: The Case for Feminist Revolution.* New York: Bantam Books.

Hamilton, Cynthia. 1988. "Alice Walker's Politics or the Politics of the Color Purple." *Journal of Black Studies* 18 (3): 379-391.

Hare, Nathan. 1964. "The Frustrated Masculinity of the Negro Male." *Negro Digest* 5-10.

Lemons, Gary. 1997. "To Be Black, Male, and Feminist-Making Womanist Space for Black men." *The International Journal of Sociology and Social Policy* 17 (1-2): 35-61.

Poussaint, Alvin. 1982. "What Every Black Woman Should Know about Black Men." *Ebony* 37 (10): 36-41.

Smith, Barbara. 1983. "Black Feminism Divorced from Black Feminist Organizing." *The Black Scholar* 14 (1): 38-45.

Stewart, James B., and Joseph W. Scott. 1978. "The Institutional Decimation of Black American Males." *Western Journal of Black Studies* 2 (2): 82-92.

Walker, Alice. 1982. *The Color Purple.* New York: Pocket Books.

—. 1993. "They Ran on Empty." *The New York Times*, May 25: A23.

Watkins, Mel. 1986. "Sex, Racism, and Black Women Writers." *The New York Times*, June 15: 1.

Williams, Joyce, and Karen A. Holmes. 1981. *The Second Assault: Rape and Public Attitudes*. Santa Barbara: Praeger.

Wolfgang, Marvin, and Franco Feracutti. 1967. *The Subculture of Violence: Towards an Integrated Theory in Criminology*. London: Tavistock Publications.

Irving Berlin: Bigotry and Brilliance

Jack Foley

Composer and lyricist Irving Berlin's Broadway credits include his 1914 Broadway debut, *Watch Your Step*, starring Vernon and Irene Castle; *The Cocoanuts* (1925) written for the Marx brothers; *Face the Music* (1932) including the hit song "Let's Have Another Cup of Coffee"; *As Thousands Cheer* (1933) including the hit songs "Heat Wave" and "Easter Parade"; *This is the Army* (1942), including the hit song "Oh How I Hate to Get Up in the Morning"; *Annie Get Your Gun* (1946); *Call Me Madam* (1950) and the 2008 limited-run Broadway version of the 1954 film *White Christmas*.

On Christmas Eve, my father had to work late at his Western Union office. We had a tree and there were presents, but I couldn't open them until he returned. The excitement was always intense. It was a mixture of desire, love, greed, and astonishment. There are people who tell children that if they are good, they will receive Christmas presents, but if they are *not* good—if they don't do what adults want them to do—they will not. This has always seemed to me a betrayal of the spirit of Christmas. Christ is the "gift," but he does not give of himself because mankind has been good. He gives of himself because mankind has been wicked and can no longer find any other means of salvation. He gives of himself because mankind has been spectacularly *bad* and has not obeyed the injunction laid down by the great authority figure, the God of the Old Testament. Christmas is one of the primary means of finding some sort of peace—even unity—between the Old and the New Testaments. Christ redeems us from the unalterable Law of the Old Testament, and the figure in whom it centers is not God the Father but God the Son. I too was a son.

Thirty years earlier, sometime in the early 1920s, my father stood on a stage somewhere outside of New York City and sang Irving Berlin's song, "All by Myself." He was stunned to discover he had stopped the show. He understood himself to be a good tap dancer but only a fair singer. "It wasn't my singing," he explained later. "The people there had never heard that song. It was Irving Berlin's song that they were applauding."

Many of Irving Berlin's songs cause a sense of wonder and amazement—a sense that an enormously familiar, even trite sentiment is being presented in a totally unexpected way. "What care I who makes the laws of a nation," Berlin wrote in 1929, paraphrasing Arius, perpetrator of the Arian

Heresy, who wrote, "Let me make a people's songs and I care not who makes their laws." Berlin:

> Let those who will take care of its rights and wrongs
> What care I who cares
> For the world's affairs
> As long as I can sing its popular songs.

That Berlin almost certainly did have opinions about "the world's affairs" is beside the point here. Citing an ancient source, Berlin is asserting his total commitment to "popular songs," a commitment that made him an extraordinarily beloved and rich man.

Unfortunately, as Irving Berlin became an all-too-familiar cultural figure—first an icon, then a dinosaur—the qualities of wonder and amazement vanished. The songs became that terrible word: *standards*. There they "stood," announcing to everyone their "excellence"—these are "good" songs, like them!—and their energy wasted away. If the early Irving Berlin, echoing a popular opinion about jazz, celebrated "Satan"—"Satan's melodies makes you want to dance forever, / And you never have to go to bed at all"—the later Irving Berlin seemed to be an embodiment of Respectability, of Republican notions. He notoriously supported the war in Vietnam. The demonic energy which fueled his early songs and made the composer an often extraordinarily difficult person (when the Allies bombed Berlin, one of Berlin's rival songwriters remarked, "They bombed the *wrong* Berlin"). This demonic energy stepped aside and took up its abode in the young, the teenaged, the rebellious, the (in the opinions of some) "simple-minded." Irving Berlin himself *couldn't stand* rock 'n' roll, and rock 'n' roll didn't give a damn about Irving Berlin. "You'll be doin' all right," crooned Elvis with just a hint of a tear and a snarl in his voice, "with your Christmas of white, but I'll have a blue—*blue blue blue*—Christmas." When Elvis actually recorded "White Christmas," Irving Berlin was furious and attempted to persuade radio stations not to play the record.

In the 1920s Jerome Kern remarked that Irving Berlin had no "place" in American music: Irving Berlin *was* American music. During Berlin's sad late years, the composer discovered to his surprise that he was *no longer* American music. His position was not unlike that of Bob Dylan—another Jewish-American performer/composer. For a few short years, Dylan seemed to be at the absolute center of the most progressive elements of American popular culture—and then he wasn't. (It's interesting that Dylan, who sometimes reworks other people's melodies to arrive at his own, demonstrated the process to an interviewer by strumming the chords to Berlin's classic "Blue Skies"—a song performed by Al Jolson in the first talking picture, *The Jazz Singer* in 1927. Berlin used "Blue Skies" again in 1946 in the film of that title, and in 1978 Willie Nelson had a hit recording of the song.)

As "Blue Skies" suggests, Berlin's songs still have considerable life in them. One hundred and thirty-one years after Irving Berlin's birth in 1888—and thirty-two years after his death in 1989 at the age of 101—it becomes possible for young Americans to hear Irving Berlin's music again and even, in Ezra Pound's phrase, to "make it new."

If we leave out the extremely significant contributions of African-American songwriters to popular music, certainly the next most prolific and successful group would have to be Jews: Berlin, Gershwin, Kern, Rodgers, Bernstein, etc. It's interesting to note that not a single one of these Jewish songwriters ever wrote a love song to a Jewish woman. Though Berlin wrote "Marie from Sunny Italy," there was no "Rachel from Jerusalem" (or in Berlin's case, more likely "Sonia from Russia") to vie with Marie. Irish composers, on the other hand—including Berlin's idol, George M. Cohan—wrote many songs about the erotic virtues of Irish women, and there were certainly songs written by Black composers about Black women. Ellington's "Tall, Tan, and Terrific" is one example. Jewish assimilation dictated that comedians such as Eddie Cantor could be explicitly Jewish—but their love interests could not. When Jewish women appear in popular songs they are figures of fun—"Second Hand Rose" or Berlin's own "Sadie Salome, Go Home" (1909): "Most ev'rybody knows / That I'm your loving Mose, / Oy, oy, oy, oy, / Where is your clothes?" We're not far here from the great African-American singer-composer, Shelton Brooks: "I'll lend you everything I've got except for my wife, / And I'll make you a present of her"—a 1910 song written by Jean C. Havez and Harry Von Tilzer and popularized by the great Black comedian, Bert Williams, whom Brooks imitated.

But if we are looking for bigotry in Berlin's work, we don't have far to go. Irving Berlin was a brilliant, complex, sometimes bigoted song-writer who produced, in addition to some of the most memorable songs ever produced by an American, a plethora of "coon songs" and min-strel numbers, including the famous "Alexander's Ragtime Band"—songs that appeared less racist in the context of the times perhaps but were racist nonetheless. The "America" that arises from his work recalls that of Alexis de Tocqueville, whose *Democracy in America* appeared in the original French and then in English translation between 1835 and 1840. In America, writes de Tocqueville, "Continual changes are ... every instant occur-ring under the observation of every man"; there is "universal tumult," an "incessant conflict of jarring interests"; "everyone is in motion." De Tocqueville's words were astonishingly prophetic. Universal tumult, jarring interests, capitalism, cit-ies, the body's need to express itself in a situation in which it is increasingly denied by metropolitan forces are all in the music that Berlin and Gershwin and many others (including African Americans like James T. Brymn—sometimes billed as "Mr. Jazz Himself"—Fats Waller, and Duke Ellington) created a hundred years after de Tocqueville published his book.

Irving Berlin's ballads reach back to different roots from his syncopated, jazz-oriented pieces—to Stephen Foster, for example. But even in Foster's distortions of African-American experience— was there ever any African American who said anything like "D Camptown ladies sing dis song, doodah, doodah"?—the plaintiveness of African-American spirituals and blues have their say: "We will sing one song for my old Kentucky home...." Isn't that song an ancestor of "White Christmas," a ballad which echoes sentimental reminiscences of "d old plantation"? "White Christmas" is anything but a "coon song"—the verse makes clear that it takes place "in Beverly Hills, L.A."!—but its sentimental invocation of "home" is not unlike those songs that located "home" in a fictional Old South. I sometimes think that without self-pity we couldn't have popular songs. Irving Berlin's ballads are marvelous examples of self-pity transformed into sound—"said" as music. Is "White Christmas" a sort of White blues? Are the "blues" in Berlin's "Blue Skies" a sort of positive answer to the great African-American genre?

How could Irving Berlin—Israel Isidore Bellin, a Jew born in Imperial Russia in 1888—write a song about the great Christian holiday, Christmas? Berlin wrote "White Christmas" in 1940, and he did with it what he had done in 1933 with another central Christian holiday, Easter. He *secularized* it. Easter is a holiday announcing Christ's resurrection. Christians celebrate it by going to church. Berlin's song, "Easter Parade," doesn't mention Christ, doesn't mention resurrection, doesn't even mention church—though the people "parading" in the song are going there. Similarly, if Christmas is a celebration of the birth of Christ, "White Christmas" doesn't say anything about that. It is a nostalgic image of an idealized holiday which perhaps never really existed. It's like the films about a typical America made by Jewish filmmakers. Did the America of Andy Hardy ever really exist? It's an America dreamed by people who were in many ways outsiders, exiles—immigrants—but who, like Berlin, were immensely successful in America. "White Christmas" accurately calls itself a "dream":

> I'm dreaming of a white Christmas
> Just like the ones I used to know
> Where the treetops glisten
> And children listen
> To hear
> Sleigh bells in the snow.
>
> I'm dreaming of a white Christmas
> With every Christmas card I write:
> "May your days be merry and bright
> And may all your Christmases be white.

That the song was sung by the unimpeachably fatherly, Irish, and *Catholic* Bing Crosby—a singer/actor who was soon to win an Academy Award for playing an Irish priest—helped it immeasurably.

In my childhood, one heard a slogan: "Let's put the Christ back in Christmas." Not in Irving Berlin's song. When he completed it, he told his secretary, "Grab your pen and take down this song. I just wrote the best song I've ever written—hell, I just wrote the best song that anybody's ever written!" It's a great song but it's a far cry from "Satan's melodies"—Berlin's term for ragtime or jazz. It's soft, sweet, if not religious exactly, infinitely nostalgic.

In its original incarnation, "White Christmas" had a verse:

> The sun is shining, the grass is green,
> The orange and palm trees sway.
> There's never been such a day
> in Beverly Hills, L.A.
> But it's December the twenty-fourth,—
> And I am longing to be up North—

But Berlin dropped the verse the moment he realized that America's soldiers were responding deeply to the song: the chorus was their dream too, but they were not likely to identify with someone who, like Irving Berlin, lived in the exclusive Beverly Hills section of L.A. The Jewish Irving Berlin probably never experienced a Christmas like the one he describes in his song, but he might have dreamed of one or visited friends who were celebrating the holiday: not a "Hanukkah Bush" but a tree that glistened with light. The I of the chorus is not the composer Irving Berlin: the I of the song is—in Delmore Schwartz's phrase—"a true blue American," a person who by definition does not carry the historical burden of being Jewish. The song is not only deeply about longing but about the possibility of assimilation as well. Many Jews were immensely successful in America but they were not quite—White.

Wikipedia: "'**White Christmas**' is a 1942 Irving Berlin song reminiscing about an old-fashioned Christmas setting. The version sung by Bing Crosby is the world's best-selling single with estimated sales in excess of 50 million copies worldwide. When the figures for other versions of the song are added to Crosby's, sales of the song exceed 100 million."

Nostalgia trumps religion. Christianity—an immense force in Western culture—constantly moves into the secular, retaining its power as imagery but removing itself from its fundamental appeal: the possibility of individual salvation. Warm and fuzzy rather than life everlasting—here, a song offered to soldiers, many of whom, as they knew very well, would die. What were they dying for? *For Christmas.*

Wikipedia: "According to [Bing] Crosby's nephew, Howard Crosby, 'I once asked Uncle

Bing about the most difficult thing he ever had to do during his entertainment career… He said in December 1944, he was in a USO show with Bob Hope and the Andrews Sisters. They did an outdoor show in northern France… he had to stand there and sing 'White Christmas' with 100,000 G.I.s in tears without breaking down himself. Of course, a lot of those boys were killed in the Battle of the Bulge a few days later."

Here is a recent poem of mine:

How can we write
Another Christmas song
When we know
That "giving" means "buying"
And "brotherhood" means "buying"—
The green not of holly but of our cash flow.

"Commercial" they say
When the season comes along
And we go
Into the stores in masses—
Lower to upper classes—
With the green not of holly but of our cash flow.

And yet you remember
A time you were told
That magic happened

In days of old,
That a god was born.

A child's sense fills you
As you buy more and more
And fall to the folly

The deep, deep folly
Of the gold-lined, frantic, fantastic, department
store...

And you sing
That giving means giving
And brotherhood means brotherhood
And you sigh
As you remember
How what once was magic
(And is magic still!)
Became a lie

(softly) Merry Christmas, Merry Christmas,
Merry Christmas
To all!

Another Jewish composer, Kurt Weill—an immigrant from Nazi Germany—faced the implications of the secularization of Christianity far more clearly than Irving Berlin. These lyrics, written by Maxwell Anderson, were sung by a Black preacher in the musical play, *Lost in the Stars*, produced on Broadway in 1949. *Lost in the Stars* was Kurt Weill's last show. This is the title song. The lyrics are excellent, but it is the music that carries the weight of the cosmic desolation that is the ultimate result of secularization. Pascal: "The eternal silence of these infinite spaces frightens me." The show is based on Alan Paton's book, *Cry the Beloved Country*. For Weill, the "beloved country" was not an idealized secular version of a Christian holiday but may well have conjured up not only South Africa, the subject of Paton's book, but his native Germany, the country he had been forced to leave. In the original production, the song was sung by Todd Duncan, who had played Porgy in the original production of Gershwin's *Porgy and Bess* (1935). As in *Porgy and Bess*—as in "White Christmas"—the lyrics carry just a hint of the minstrel show even as they attempt to move well beyond it.

> Before Lord God made the Sea and the Land
> He held all the stars in the palm of his hand
> And they ran through his fingers like grains of sand
> And one little star fell alone
>
> Then the Lord God hunted through the wide night air
> For the little dark star on the wind down there
> And he stated and promised He'd take special care
> So it wouldn't get lost again
>
> Now a man don't mind if the stars grow dim
> And the clouds blow over and darken him
> So long as the Lord God's watching over them
> Keeping track how it all goes on—
>
> But I've been walking through the night and the day
> Till my eyes get weary and my head turns grey
> And sometimes it seems maybe God's gone away
> Forgetting His promise that we heard him say
> And we're lost out here in the stars
>
> Little stars, big stars
> Blowing through the night...

And we're lost out here in the stars
Little stars, big stars
Blowing through the night...

(CHORUS)

And we're lost
And we're lost
And we're lost
And we're lost

(SOLOIST)

And we're lost
Out here in the stars

"Home" is, precisely, a space in which we are not "lost." Berlin was an immigrant, and an immigrant may be defined as a person caught between two "homes." His songs are a magnificent attempt to bridge the gap between ancient Russia (and all that meant) and the USA. As a child he witnessed his first "home" (in Russia) totally destroyed in a pogrom. "White Christmas" conjures a new home, as does Berlin's "God Bless America": "my home sweet home." The latter song was suggested as a replacement for our hard-to-sing national anthem. It's said that Berlin's song was refused because Berlin was Jewish. Irving Berlin came to America as a child and was a great success at "writing its popular songs." But he learned as well that there were certain lines that he as a Jew could not cross. He gave America dreams, including its dream of the fake "Negro," the minstrel, and of a totally secularized holy day, but if in a way he was a sterling example of the American Dream, he was also subject to the bigotry at the heart of American entertainment: he was a Jew and a Jew—no matter what he wrote, no matter how much money he made—was never, even at Christmas, "White."

Neither Cockeyed nor an Optimist about *South Pacific*

Emil Guillermo

If Ensign Nellie Forbush, USN is the cockeyed optimist, make me the modern Asian-American pessimist. Though *South Pacific* has been hailed ever since it came on the scene in 1949 as Rodgers' and Hammerstein's antidote to bigotry, I remain unmoved. It was never an antidote to anything of the sort.

Rather it was an enabler, that flashed its own toned-down bigotry for a mostly privileged White theatre audience of its day. And the audience got just what it wanted—toothsome tunes to forget their troubles while sipping a Mai-Tai fantasy.

South Pacific is the story of a mostly White military waiting idly in the wings to fight a war fueled by xenophobia. At its core, *South Pacific* is about Americans in a foreign conflict made tolerable by dueling love stories and beautiful songs that are now part of the American Songbook. That part is undeniable.

But in *South Pacific* love doesn't triumph over all. War is not averted in favor of a peacetime love-in. The war finally kicks in and conveniently claims the life of one of the musical's heroes who may have gone too far in his interracial coupling. Was Lieutenant Joe Cable's death a coincidence or consequence of his love of the Polynesian Liat? It essentially turns into a pandering message to Whites, not a condemnation of bigotry, but also a warning that interracial love leads to ruin, not celebration.

Compared to the musical's main event, the love story of Nellie and Emile, White status is never threatened or compromised, but restored and preserved. People of color remain subjugated in the ways people of color were always subjugated in those days—as servile or infantile (in this case, literally).

It has to be said that the sexist overtones of Post-World War II America are at times even more cringeworthy than the racist ones in *South Pacific*. While the White women are all "dames" and objectified as such, it's countered with the image of the strong conniving woman, "Bloody Mary," played with a menacing charm by the late actress, Juanita Hall, an African American in real life who could pass as a dark-skinned Polynesian. It's like a casting precursor to *Hamilton*, only here it's replacing a fringe "other"—an obscure Pacific Islander—with a Black who passes for Asian. (Is that Kosher?) Or is "Asian" the gateway drug cure-all for all racism? A half-step or shade at a time? Curiously, other than Hall, I didn't see any Black faces in this anti-bigotry tale. Asian was just easier to handle in 1949.

From her intro set piece to her alluring "Bali Hai," Bloody Mary makes things happen in *South Pacific*. She's the charming grass-skirt dealer who sees pimping her young daughter to an officer as the best opportunity to a better life for her family.

In sum, we have a grand confection of a musical, sprinkled with a bit of troubling bigotry, but nothing that challenges the realm of acceptable American racist behavior too much, not even in the '40s or '50s and certainly not now.

Indeed, the show is barely woke by today's standards. Today's general audience would shudder at any mention of the "N" word. Unless it were produced by Jay-Zee. *South Pacific* captures the hate of the day with the casual use of the "J" word for the Japanese enemy. Back then, saying "Jap" to show a jingoistic hate and disrespect of the Japanese was ubiquitous in society. Doesn't make it right, not as Japanese Americans were imprisoned in horse barns and other isolated camps in one of the darkest periods of America's racist history. *South Pacific*'s libretto is littered with the "J" word.

By 1958, the musical was turned into a practically pre-psychedelic movie dripping in punch bowl color. Also directed by Joshua Logan, the film had some of the same actors, notably Hall's Bloody Mary. But in less than ten years the script changed the "J" word to the full word, "Japanese," or it simply eliminated it from some passages. Progress?

Seeing *South Pacific* go from Broadway to film is like noticing all the lumps under yesterday's Oriental rug.

As mild as the show's attempt at exposing ugly bigotry was, some people were threatened by even the suggestion of interracial marriage. Hard to imagine this about a musical whose calling card is "Some Enchanted Evening." There were protests during the national road tour in Georgia in 1953 when White audiences complained about the love story involving the White military nurse (Nellie Forbush) and a French plantation owner (Emile de Becque) who had mixed race children from a previous marriage. Theater writer Andrea Most wrote that the protests were led by Georgia politicians who were part of the anti-Communist fervor of post-WWII and the House Un-American Activities Committee. They saw inter-marriage as linked to communism and a threat to America, and tried to blunt the musical's popularity as anti-American. It was love's red scare.

I Am Not Emile

When I was a young adult, older friends who knew of *South Pacific* would tease me about de Becque's being an Emile. Like me. It was just rare to see any-one like me on any Broadway or film production.

A name was close enough.

But *South Pacific* was never meant for me. My parents were Filipino-American immigrants from a little further west of the musical's island setting. I was born during the years in between the play's Broadway debut in 1949 and the 1958 movie. I was not its target demographic.

The play was intended for the Nellie Forbushes in the audience, to have their consciences rocked, in order to consider such things as people who are the "other" as real people. That's Nellie's and Lieutenant Cable's story. Certainly, it's not the story of Emile's servants, Henry or Marcel. Bit parts, but they always seemed big to me.

They reminded me of my father.

I wish I could say all I know about race and intermarriage I learned from Rodgers and Hammerstein. But that would be a lie.

We didn't need the real *South Pacific*. We had our own Asian-Caucasian issues right here at home. My father, Emiliano Guillermo, born in 1906—in America's first colony, the Philippines—arrived as an American national in 1928, just in time for the Great Depression. By 1930, 30,000 Filipino men were in the U.S., mostly in California, in male to female ratios of 14-1 due to the demand for common labor. Whites claimed the Filipinos took not only jobs, but their White women. It created a sexual jealousy and tension that resulted in race-mixing with Filipinos being killed, and even lynched in California.

On top of that were racist laws that prevented land ownership and racial intermarriage. Most Filipinos could not start a family until the middle 1950s when, after the war, more Filipino women were allowed into the U.S. A whole generation passed before my father was able to meet and marry my mother.

I see Emile's servants and it reminded me of my dad who served wealthy diners in restaurants and hotels during the height of *South Pacific*'s fame. I wonder how many of them wanted to call him Henry or Marcel? Or ever even wondered if he had a name. Filipinos had their own WWII issues as the Philippines was a key theater of battle for Gen. Douglas MacArthur. As the war progressed to the Philippines, FDR called on Filipinos to fight alongside the U.S. in exchange for citizenship and benefits. Thousands of Filipinos answered the call, only to have the promise reneged by the U.S. with the Rescission Act of 1946. Some veterans are still waiting to be made whole. It's a historical pattern I thought of as I read the libretto and saw the lines of Henry, Marcel or Emile's young mixed-race kids.

They weren't invisible to me.

I also knew Emile was not Emil. Emile de Becque was from the colonial French ruling class. Not some Asian or Polynesian success story, or a privileged person of color—someone who could be played by, say, the Rock, (half-Black, half-Samoan, perhaps a modern Juanita Hall). Emile is definitely White. It makes the relationship with Nellie Forbush not so odd. Quite natural even. Colonizers attract.

Emile is also a man who is running away from a secret past, from bullies in his native France, he says, who finds himself on an island, where he meets Nellie, his true love, a blonde "hick from the sticks," Little Rock. She's equally out of place on a much bigger rock in a south of a different kind, trying to undo her upbringing.

And so we have a new equation brewing, of geography and class, where we're all searching for that one "thing" on some enchanted evening.

An odd moment comes early in Act One when Nellie reveals she's not concerned about Emile's age, or his foreignness. She doesn't even care that Emile has confessed that he is a murderer.

"You have just told me that you killed a man and that it's all right," Nellie tells him. "I hardly know you, and yet I know it's all right."

That's all right? OK with murder? Nellie Forbush would have been an ideal O.J. juror!

She is not, however, OK with Emile having children with a woman of color. Nellie doesn't ever mention race. She doesn't come out and object to Emile being with a Polynesian woman. Instead, she states her objection to the "woman you had before—her color…"

Color mixing. Miscegenation. It was worse than murder. It was the killing off of the White race, and provides the subtext of White supremacy at play. Nellie surmises she can't help her bigotry; she was born that way. Not like Lady Gaga. More like David Duke. But as the song goes, that's not necessarily the case.

Cut to the show's most important song, the preachy, evidentiary proclamation.

"You've got to be carefully taught," provides the play's insight and the key message. You're not born with racism; "It happens after you're born," sings Lt. Joe Cable. "You've got to be taught to be afraid. Of people whose eyes are oddly made. And people whose skin is a different shade. You have to be carefully taught."

If only we could sing away racism.

Still Hummable at a BLM March Near You?

That's the problem with the show more than 70 years later.

It leaves us with a few good songs for a Karaoke night among people of a certain age. But *South Pacific* is not the song book of a revolution.

No one was singing "Carefully Taught" during the civil rights surge in 1964 or 1965. Or when the cities burned around the country during that decade. Or when the anti-war marches began.

Can you imagine Martin Luther King Jr. at the March on Washington breaking into "Happy Talk":

"You got to have a dream, if you don't have a dream, how you going to have a dream come true?"

Me neither.

In today's world, these Rodgers and Hammerstein ditties barely pass for pre-historic diversity training. But let's be fair. They are locked in a time and intended for latent and blatant White racists to reconsider their feelings. They weren't songs to rise up a populace.

Because of that, more than seven decades later, no matter how many times the show's been revived in the last 12 years, it just seems like a dated relic, a sad tribute to the snail-paced evolution of our country's racial mindset. Just a marker on choppy ocean waters, way south of Hawaii.

The tunes are still toothsome. And even I admit to humming, "Happy Talk" as I write. But relevant? Maybe if Chance the Rapper and Justin Bieber did an update? Or Kanye West and Taylor Swift?

South Pacific made bigotry and the fight against it entertaining enough in its day for Broadway. I just don't expect to see anyone humming "You've got to Be Carefully Taught," at a BLM march anytime soon.

It would have to be some enchanted protest.

The Book of Mormon Is Racist—Why Isn't Anyone Talking about It?*

Claire J. Harris

When I saw *The Book of Mormon*, all I knew was that everybody loved it—from Oprah Winfrey to Jon Stewart. One of the most successful musicals of all time, the show has won nine Tony Awards and grossed over $500 million. It is also incredibly racist. Yes, I know the Mormons aren't a race. I'm talking about the Ugandans.

I had no idea the story was even set in Uganda, or I probably would have thought twice before buying a ticket. Instead, I spent $100 to feel horrendously uncomfortable in a theatre full of White people laughing uproariously as one racist trope was rolled out after another. Although my urge was to leave at the interval, I went back in hoping

* Previously published on Claire Harris's website: https://www.clairejharris.com/2018/11/10/the-book-of-mormon-is-racist/; medium.com; and thebigsmoke.com

the musical would somehow cleverly undermine the stereotypes it had set up.

The most self-aware moment is when the two White missionaries gleefully claim to be as African as Bono during a song called "I am Africa." They go on to list a complete range of African stereotypes: "Zulu spear," "running barefoot," "primitive," endowed," and more. The problem is, the narrative does not critique these caricatures but serves only to reinforce them.

When I emerged two hours later and went home to google "Book of Mormon racist," I trawled through the rave reviews and found next to nothing. Since almost everyone I know has seen this musical, I asked others whether they felt the same. Here were the most common responses.

"What do you mean, racist?"

The events take place in Uganda but they could be anywhere in the continent. Africa is shorthand for an undeveloped and backward place, as represented by mud huts and semi-naked villagers. The show lazily relies on repeated jokes: the most common being a female character who sends text messages on a typewriter. Cue audience laughter. Every. Single. Time.

This character is the only Ugandan we care about but I have no idea what her name is because the Mormons refer to her as things like "Nicotine" and "Nutell." The audience roars with laughter because isn't it funny how unpronounceable foreign names are? She is highly fetishized, particularly through a baptism scene with a Mormon missionary that is layered with sexual innuendo.

At least she is a sympathetic character. The other Ugandans are non-descript fools who are all riddled with AIDS (the audience shrieks with laughter!) and believe that raping babies will rid them of it. When the missionaries convince them to have sex with frogs instead, the audience hoots. Another running gag is a character's ongoing complaint that he has maggots in his scrotum. Fetch the doctor? He IS the doctor! Because African medicine LOL.

"But it makes fun of Mormons!"

Everybody has been so busy analyzing whether or not the show is offensive to Mormons that the conversation about Ugandans has been non-existent. While the narrative certainly pokes fun at Mormon beliefs, its characterization of the missionaries is wholly affectionate.

More than this, the Mormons are the clear heroes of the story in a classic White savior ending whereby the Americans save the village from the neighboring warlord General Butt-F***ing Naked (hilarity at each mention of his name) who is trying to circumcise all the local women. Indeed, the villagers create a new religion around the missionaries themselves, who have lifted them out of their state of godlessness and un-enlightenment. Thank God for colonialism—in this case literally.

The Mormons themselves have actually done rather well out of the musical, reportedly standing outside theatres with flyers and benefiting from a spike in conversions. So the answer to this is… not really.

"Well yeah, haven't you seen South Park?"

Because I've never watched the TV show, I don't know what so-called "equal opportunity offensiveness" looks like. However, I have been appalled by people who consider themselves progressive and yet are defending jokes about Africans (because Uganda is interchangeable with anywhere else) being rapists, AIDS-ridden, savage, simple, and in need of saving by White Americans.

Perhaps it's too much to expect a musical by the creators of *South Park* to accurately assess the impact of the Mormon missionary movement and other religious evangelism in non-Western countries. But why did it have to be set in Uganda at all?

I cannot understand why the argument "it's their style of humor, of course it's irreverent" is able to wash in 2018—especially while in the rest of the entertainment industry there has been a (rightful) push for greater inclusion of diverse voices to combat racial stereotypes.

The caricatures in *The Book of Mormon* look exactly the same as those that have been perpetuated for centuries. They are not only careless, they are dangerous—and yet they have done nothing to stop the juggernaut success of this show. I can only imagine how it would make an African audience member feel. Unsurprisingly, there didn't seem to be any.

Why *Butterfly* Should Stop Committing Literary Hara-kiri

Yuri Kageyama

Sex is often about violence. It is often, unfortunately, more about the question of whom one has chosen to subjugate than about love. A fetish.

The Japanese woman portrayed in Giacomo Puccini's early 1900s opera *Madame Butterfly* is that fetish supreme, a doll to be played with, then forgotten, a no-strings-attached consumable object of transient lust.

She waits and waits and waits, selfless, full of trust and forgiveness.

The White male isn't ever held accountable, except in reproachful looks and gasps of singsong horror.

The woman of color drinks in her oppression in a swooning soprano of submission.

In a fitting metaphor, she blindfolds her half-White son.

She kills herself, stabbing herself with the hara-kiri dagger of her father, symbolic of the dead-end pagan society of her ancestors.

To be fair, according to the script, Butterfly is only 15 when she meets her White prince on a white horse.

Benjamin Franklin Pinkerton, an American, lands in the port city of Nagasaki, southwestern Japan, the archetypal tourist on a roam, searching for sex galore.

He is not disappointed. He gets a dream-vacation house, complete with sliding screen doors and bowing servants, for a pittance. And so why not?

She is in a weak position from the start. She is a geisha, basically a poverty-stricken whore in kimono. Her options for advancement are few.

No attractive Japanese men want her, only those who resemble banzai-screaming soldiers.

There is no role for Ken Watanabe, who played the lead to a White woman in caricatured musical theater, *The King and I*, Lee Byung-hun, Bruce Lee, BTS or other heartthrobs.

There is only Pinkerton. He varies in size, looks, and interpretation, some more remorseful than others, but not in race.

You may argue all males have done the Pinkerton number on females, regardless of race. You may argue the story reflects modern history. After World War II, American soldiers left Japanese women pregnant with their children. Some went to America, known as "war brides." Others became real-life Butterflies.

Despite Puccini's foresight into such realities, he clearly had no real knowledge of Japan.

His musical references and depictions are those of an imaginary Japan, unabashedly inaccurate, showing no qualms at freewheeling appropriation.

This is a Japan where people file in small-stepped shuffles, carrying transparent umbrellas, bowing rigidly like statues.

He is telling his story, not theirs. And he does his storytelling well, perhaps too well.

The experience of betrayal and lost love is powerfully universal. The audience's empathy with that experience transcends race. And there is the music.

But his story, being his, is one-sided, a wet dream for the mainstream psyche, limiting the other race in its entirety to a demeaning, cardboard existence.

In some productions, Asian actors got cast, proving the play has provided opportunities for talented non-Westerners in Western theater. But that is incidental.

Actors playing the Japanese roles are mostly White, sometimes with odd makeup, white plastered all over their faces, and black eyeliner spiking upward at the corners of their eyes, accentuating so-called slanted eyes.

The images of subordination are brutal. As her name implies, she is a butterfly, collected and pinned in a box for the White male to gawk at.

To her, he is the sun, tall and strong, a god with a carefree laugh.

He is the white ship, entering Nagasaki harbor, as gloriously and triumphantly as a penis enters a vagina, guns thundering.

She is the forlorn delicate victim, happily scattering flowers to welcome him back, filling her house with honeyed sweetness. The lord has returned. Little does she know he has a White wife.

She had been a diversion, that Chinese or sushi takeout for now and then, on those nights when you're tired of steak or pasta.

When Butterfly sings that famous aria about her never-dying belief in Pinkerton's return, her face turns psychotic with make-believe.

She does not raise questions. She does not wrest fate out of its trenches and turn the story into something else.

In an alternate story, Butterfly renames herself Godzilla. Or Mothra, if you want to stay within the categorical imagery.

She breathes the fire of revenge and takes the dagger of racial justice and stabs Pinkerton and his smug-faced White wife the moment they enter her quaint Japanese house.

She digs a big hole in the backyard, dumps their bodies and grows chrysanthemums and rice in the garden, fertilized well by their fermenting bodies.

She does not blindfold her son.

She raises him to be proud of his bicultural origins. He studies all kinds of literature and the sciences. He models himself after Thurgood Marshall.

She teaches him that objectification of people and appropriation of a culture are wrong. He learns all people are created equal.

The Suzie Wong typecasting of Asian womanhood has been that tiny window of appearance in the mainstream mindset for decades.

Even today, as the world globalizes, it is still the White storyteller, the modern-day Puccini, at the steering wheel as he goes across the world, Pinkerton-style.

The Japanese housekeeper has merely gone global in Marie Kondo, giving mundane common-sensical tips with glamorous but pigeonholed fanfare.

We're still buying into the modern-day Butterfly stereotype, except maybe at Roppongi clubs, where the special "gaijin" status is flaunted, Pinkerton-style.

Adding to the complexity, White women are also buying into the setup, pretending to become Japanese housewives, doing their own pigeon-toed dance, like the White actresses playing Japanese in *Madame Butterfly*, speaking broken Japanese, a Karen abroad, assured of being no longer ugly in communities of color, where Whiteness guarantees superiority.

Even as White America grapples with the challenges of Black Lives Matter, the presence of Asians in America remains as limited in the political conversation as it is in theater and other realms of art.

In Hollywood and other mass entertainment, the Asian is the random grocery-store owner who speaks pidgin. The cook. The laundry worker. The gardener. The engineer or the mathematician, at best. Or that prostitute and wife.

In American society, the lawyer and the doctor are those roles children of immigrant and minority families work hard to excel in school to win.

He is that police officer who looks around nervously holding his gun, as that White policeman presses his knee against George Floyd's neck for more than eight minutes.

The role we land is never the storyteller. Never the literati. Never the conductor of the important music. Never the president of the United States.

We aren't front-page news. We aren't invited to that evolving potentially explosive, game-changing, history-in-the-making conversation between White and Black.

We are truly the Other, banned forever from the spotlight, a butterfly fluttering outside a shut screen.

We are that invisible race, and, yes, we have sought to be invisible, proving we are 100 percent American, not causing waves, not rocking the White boat, being the model minority, law-abiding, tax-paying, obedient.

That is the story of Butterfly, "cho-cho-sahn," pronounced with a drawl, although, in all my years,

I have never met a Japanese with such a ridiculous name.

Being reduced to a category—race, gender, nationality, ethnic group—stripped of individual traits and personhood, underlines the suffering of discrimination.

It encapsulates the bigger-than-life stories thrown at us, masquerading as the arts, academia, role models, success stories and definition of humanity.

It seeps into our minds, scarring us for life. The pain gets passed down generations.

It is the cruel personal fallout from systemic racism, that same systemic racism that can project how long you live, how much money you make, how well you might avoid prison-time, how much happiness you claim.

It is time we stop turning the dagger on ourselves, and we instead courageously claim our own voice, even if no one will listen.

We must use the dagger to kill that tired old fake-Kabuki story.

We must sing our own Butterfly Aria:

One fine day you'll find me
A thread of belief arising .
In my Self
Where it always lay waiting
And then
I will be free
***

Then the chains will come off
No longer enslaved, silenced
We define who we are
See me? I don't need anyone.
***

I do not go to meet him
Not I
I at last understand what he has meant
Not waiting
Or even remembering;
I control my fate
Define my sexuality
***

Our struggles of history;
We can end
Someone else telling our story,
To gain equality
***

Can you guess who we are?
And when we've reached the summit
Can you guess what we'll say?
We will call out, "We matter,"
From within our hearts
***

We wait not for answers,
We stand for our own lives,
We write our own poems.
***

One fine day you'll find me
A thread of belief arising
In my Self
Where it always lay waiting
And then
I will be free

***

This will all come to pass as I tell you
Banish your idle fears
For I will be free
I know

The Unbearable Whiteness of *Oklahoma!**

In new Broadway revival, the blinding sunshine of the Territory exposes violence beneath the romantic myth

Soraya Nadia McDonald

Though it hasn't always been acknowledged, Rodgers and Hammerstein's *Oklahoma!* has always been a musical about Whiteness.

This is important because a new and well-reviewed production is now running on Broadway. *Oklahoma!* has often been summarized through a lens of racial neutrality as a romantic musical about a woman named Laurey Williams trying to make a choice between two suitors: Jud Fry, a hard-working farmhand who lives in the smokehouse of a farm owned by Laurey and her Aunt Eller. And guitar-strumming Curly McClain, who is more socially adept, but doesn't offer much beyond a pretty face. Set in the Claremore Indian Territory of Oklahoma in 1906, *Oklahoma!* delivers a rose-tinted view of history that centers on happy White people whose greatest concern is a town dance that will raise money to build a new school. It's a classic example of willful erasure and ahistorical mythmaking.

In 1838 and 1839, President Andrew Jackson forced thousands of Native Americans to abandon their homes east of the Mississippi. Even though Oklahoma was the end point of the genocidal forced migration known as the Trail of Tears, *Oklahoma!* doesn't feature a single Native American character. In fact, its only explicitly non-White character is Ali Hakim, a Persian peddler who seeks romantic encounters that don't come with marital status.

Director Daniel Fish's new, stripped-down revival of *Oklahoma!* doesn't play by those rules, though. In this version, now running at Circle in the Square Theater through Jan. 19, Laurey is played by a Black woman, Rebecca Naomi Jones. Laurey's best friend, Ado Annie, is played by Ali Stroker, who uses a wheelchair, the first actress to do so on a Broadway stage. When Stroker won the Tony for best actress in a featured role in a musical in June, she was the first performer who uses a wheelchair to be nominated, much less win.

Suffice it to say, this ain't your granny's *Oklahoma!* The musical, which won the 2019 Tony for best revival, has been popularly characterized as "Sexy *Oklahoma!*" That's largely because of the horny howling of its handsome leading man, Damon Daunno, who plays Curly, and its shamelessly libidinous Ado Annie. But I did not find *Oklahoma!* to be sexy so much as darkly terrifying—and I mean that in a good way.

That's because this version, which faithfully maintains the original script and lyrics of the 1943 musical while updating the orchestrations with modern arrangements, subjects toxic Whiteness and masculinity to the glaring bleach of the noonday sun.

The revival is unique because of its deft interrogation of the Whiteness and toxic masculinity that has long been romanticized in the American western, and in the many treacly iterations of *Oklahoma!* that have been mounted since 1943. This version asks its audience to consider a familiar world in an unfamiliar way: through the eyes of a Black woman with little to no physical security or power of her own.

The first thing one notices upon entering Circle in the Square is the aggressive brightness of the room's lighting (more than a few members of the audience wore sunglasses through the performance). The second is that the walls are lined with racks upon racks upon racks of shotguns.

The lighting turns out to be subversive. Much like a black light held over the surfaces of a sketchy motel room, it illuminates all the ickiness lurking on surfaces that appear otherwise innocuous. It welcomes you to the Oklahoma territory, where flowers fill the prairie and the June bugs zoom, and then it ensures that you cannot turn away from the ugliness that lurks there. "Everything's going my way" certainly applies to the men of the Territory. But its female residents? Not so much.

It's strange to see *Oklahoma!* when the horrors of mass shootings (most recently in Dayton, Ohio, and El Paso, Texas) are still in the shallow recesses of one's consciousness. But mostly, I was reminded of violence specifically linked to virulent misogyny, and so Alek Minassian, Elliot Rodger, and George Sodini entered my mind within minutes of the introduction of Jud (Patrick Vaill). Minassian, Rodgers, and Sodini are White men who committed mass murder because they were angry, lonely, and felt entitled to attention from women when they weren't getting it. Minassian identifies as an "incel," or involuntary celibate.

There is a rhythm to the news of mass shootings, and one beat in particular is frustrating metronomic: The killers, more often than not, have a history of abuse or antipathy toward women. In *Oklahoma!*, Jud is armed with an unshakeable crush, a shifty attitude, and a revolver. Vaill imbues Jud with a patina of gentle shyness, underneath which beats a familiar pulse of resentment, entitlement, and a violent temper precariously held in check. Jud might be an excellent farmhand, but he is not a good man. It makes for a terribly dangerous combination for Laurey.

To survive in the modern world, women develop a spidey sense about men who would potentially harm us, and we mold our lives around the avoidance of male aggression. We move to a different subway car if someone stares a little too long, or brushes up a little too close. We slow our gait to let someone pass rather than take the chance that he may be following when we must walk late at night. And we get very good at managing—managing expectations, managing tempers, and managing egos.

The same reality of ever-present male danger is true for the women of the Territory. For them, the most effective way to guard against it is to get married. (Nothing sucks the romance out of courtship quite like knowing you're seeking a man in hopes that his presence will prevent your rape or murder.) Laurey has a decision to make about who she will choose for the dance and her life afterward: Curly or Jud? By Laurey's second interaction with the seemingly mild-mannered Jud, I felt my stomach grow queasy with worry. Oda Mae Brown from *Ghost* made an entrance in my notebook: "Laurey," I wrote furiously, "You in danger, girl!"

Before Fish reimagined her, Laurey was usually portrayed as a lucky woman blessed with a surfeit of romantic possibilities. Nowhere is that more clear than in Fred Zinnemann's 1955 film adaptation. In Zinnemann's *Oklahoma!*, Laurey is played by Shirley Jones, a sunny, self-assured blonde whose good looks, tiny waist, and homespun charm are enough to tame any man.

When Shirley Jones sings "Many A New Day," she's surrounded by White women pirouetting in bloomers and petticoats, and she's laying out a philosophy that Ellen Fein and Sherrie Schneider would come to monetize some four decades later in *The Rules*, possibly the worst self-help book about dating ever published. Essentially, it is a doctrine that tells women that all their power and moral authority lie in their sexual availability or lack thereof, also known as playing hard to get.

But this display of performative reluctance isn't an indication of power, so much as the lack of it, especially when you consider the presence of armed threats like Jud. From the beginning of the musical, Aunt Eller is telling Curly how much her niece likes him, no matter how much Laurey's behavior indicates the opposite. It's strategic: Aunt Eller's trying to provide some security for Laurey, in the limited way that she can, by playing matchmaker. Sexual violation is a constant threat for women, even for Ado Annie, who is generally portrayed as a ditsy, well-meaning slut with her rendition of the song "I Cain't Say No."

Stroker's Ado Annie, on the other hand, delivers a rollicking, proudly sex positive rendition of the song, a recognition of the character's agency.

Still, in both scenarios, Ado Annie's choices are protected by her father's ever-present shotgun–to a point. She may get around, and she may like it, but she's still got to marry *somebody*, and furthermore, someone with money. Ado Annie's father insists that a man vying for her affections have at least $50 to his name before he'll let him marry her. (Remember, it's 1906.)

Laurey doesn't really have two viable options so much as she's faced with making a choice between a man who will almost certainly kill her if he doesn't get what he wants and a well-meaning dunce who thinks the height of being gentlemanly means getting down to the dirty business of dispatching the Territory's resident incel. Jones is not the only member of the *Oklahoma!* company who is Black, but her Blackness serves to reinforce just how vulnerable and disenfranchised Laurey is in a place where men hold an overwhelming amount of sociopolitical power and women have nearly none. That social order is enforced and maintained with guns:

- When Ali Hakim won't commit to Ado Annie, her father threatens him with a shotgun.
- When Jud and Curly want to intimidate each other, they shoot holes into the roof and wall of the smokehouse.

- When Laurey finds herself in need of protection from one bad man, it comes from another wielding—you guessed it—a gun.

Jones plays Laurey as a woman moving through the world with tense, uneasy reluctance. At times, she exhibits an attraction to Curly, but it never seems to permeate too deeply, perhaps with the exception of the dream ballet (danced with magnetic athleticism by Gabrielle Hamilton) that explores Laurey's subconscious. It concludes with Laurey's id scooching crotch first offstage toward Curly—she's made her "choice."

But even when Laurey agrees to marry Curly and enters the stage in her wedding dress, she's bereft of the glowing, floaty ebullience typically associated with brides. Instead, the subtle hesitations in Jones' movements and the drawn expression of her face leaves the viewer wishing poor Laurey had a trusted maid of honor to ask, "You OK, sis? I got the horses in the back if you want to ride east 'til we can't ride no more." It's a beautifully crafted performance, full of simmering internal contradictions that Laurey dare not raise aloud. She seems more resigned than anything to spend her life with Curly, if only because he provides protection from the Juds of the world and she knows that she needs it.

I could not help but see parallels between Laurey and the protagonist of *Test Pattern*, a new film from director Shatara Michelle Ford that premiered earlier this year at BlackStar Film Festival and is currently seeking distribution. *Test Pattern* explores the aftermath of sexual assault for a Black woman living in Austin, Texas, named Renesha. Renesha (Brittany S. Hall) is in a loving interracial relationship when she is sexually assaulted during a celebratory night out with a friend. (Coincidentally, the two works share an actor; Will Brill plays Hakim in *Oklahoma!* and Renesha's boyfriend Evan in *Test Pattern*.) Like Laurey, Renesha ends up spending a great deal of time managing the emotions of two White men, one of whom is ostensibly "good" and the other who is "bad." It turns out the two men are not so different. Like Jud and Curly, they both prioritize their own wants over the needs of the Black woman who is the object of their desire or devotion. This is not accidental. In both the Territory of 1906 and modern-day Austin, the world is constructed to serve these men, and that's what they've come to expect. This is their version of neutral.

Oklahoma! becomes a jaunty horror show when Laurey is splattered with Jud's blood on her wedding day after Curly guns him down and the entire company belts out a lively rendition of "Oklahoma." The residents of the territory ignore the cancer infecting their community in favor of singing, dancing, and the avoidance of discomfort, in much the same way that no amount of tragic death seems to spur meaningful action on gun control.

Ultimately, *Oklahoma!* provides a nuanced opportunity for audiences to reexamine systems of power from the view of those least protected by them. The artists will even serve you chili and cornbread during the show's intermission. The timing is key—better to eat a bowl before Jud is daid, when its contents can't remind you of his bullet-blasted innards.

Everyone Tells My *West Side Story* but Me

Nancy Mercado, PhD

"The more things change, the more they stay the same..."

Jean-Baptiste Alphonse Karr

Was it the latest mass migration of Puerto Ricans after hurricane Maria to the United States mainland that did it? After six decades and many, many revivals, *West Side Story* will premiere yet again in the form of a Spielberg motion picture. Shakespeare's famed *Romeo and Juliet* love story set amidst 1950's urban warring gangs in New York City: Puerto Ricans against Whites.

The origins of *West Side Story* are interesting if not revealing of the story's true nature. Created during the McCarthy era and years before Gay Liberation by four White queer Jewish men in the early 1950s: Arthur Laurents, Leonard Bernstein, Jerome Robbins and Stephen Sondheim, "[t]he musical's origin story is one of displaced ethnicity," much like the displacement *West Side Story*'s creators must have felt (Pollack-Pelzner). It's known that Jerome Robbins "was deeply conflicted about his Jewish roots and terrified at being outed as gay by the House Un-American Activities Committee [and that] Arthur Laurents was blacklisted during the Joseph McCarthy hearings. Sondheim always regretted the song, 'I Feel Pretty.' [Discomforted by the] feeling that he had revealed too much of himself in lines such as 'I feel pretty and witty and gay' and 'I'm in love with a pretty wonderful boy'" (Pollack-Pelzner).

Initially titled *The East Side Story*, its creators included warring factions that involved Jews against Catholics that was changed to Whites against Mexicans and finally to Whites against Puerto Ricans living on the West Side of New York City. The original Broadway theater production happened after the 1940's mass migration of Puerto Ricans onto the US mainland. Changes to Puerto Rico's political and thus its economic structure; the election of Luis Muñoz Marin (of Estado Libre Asociado de Puerto Rico fame)* into the island's Senate and the appointment by the United States

---

Rivera, Magaly. "Welcome to Puerto Rico!" https://welcome.topuertorico.org/reference/ela.shtml. 1 December, 2020. The term was first used by Puerto Rico in 1952 as "Commonwealth of Puerto Rico". The name in Spanish for Puerto Rico is "Estado Libre Asociado de Puerto Rico" ("Free Associated State of Puerto Rico").

of Rexford Guy Tugwell as the island's governor set the industrialization of the island into motion and the displacement of a major part of its population (Rivera). Puerto Rican families were divided as some family members remained on the island while others migrated in mass to the US mainland in search of work. Their island agricultural way of life and its economy had been dismantled by U.S. capitalists' interests intending to exploit the island's resources and its people via industrialization. Migrating to the U.S. was in the majority of instances, a heartbreaking experience. Leaving family and the comforts of a tropical island home for dilapidated cold urban cities covered in English was at minimum, an alienating experience on ascending levels.

Notwithstanding the musical's genius in its libretto, music and choreography, racism and stereotypes in *West Side Story* occur on various dimensions. This happens as part of the production process as well as being embedded in the story's essence itself. Many may know the famous story about the use of "brown face" during the 1961 filming of this play; "brown face" used on White actors hired to portray Puerto Rican gang members. Even the couple of Puerto Ricans used in the film were splattered with thick brown makeup to authenticate their Puerto Ricaness. Rita Moreno is famous for "complaining about how inauthentically dark her makeup was, and at one point confronting the makeup artist about it. He looked at her aghast and asked, 'What, are you racist?'" (Fallon). Was it unbeknownst to Arthur Laurents that Puerto Ricans come in all colors, shapes and sizes?

In Von Hove's 2020 Broadway revival, Puerto Ricans are lumped together with Mexicans as if we're all the same. While I have the utmost respect for my Mexican sisters and brothers, the fact remains, we are not the same culture. "When Anita disparages her birth island—'always the hurricanes blowing, always the population growing'—the audience sees news footage of Hurricane Maria devastating San Juan. At the end of the song [Von Hove displays] a long aerial tracking shot [of] the border wall with Mexico." Similarly, "as the Sharks sing, 'immigrant goes to America,' the Broadway Theatre back wall displays video footage of Mexican immigrants splashing across the Rio Grande" (Pollack-Pelzner). "Van Hove has [also] diversified the traditionally all-White Jets with a majority Black cast. But that's a muddled change: Why do the Black Jets seem to feel more solidarity with their White fellows than with the Puerto Rican Sharks" (Grady)? As a writer, I too have an affinity for artistic license but, give me a break. This isn't any kind of license but more a type of neglect or maybe just frivolity. Jesus! I hope Von Hove is intelligent enough to know the difference between Puerto Ricans and Mexicans and if he's not, who "courageously" gave him the use of a Broadway theatre?

Instances of type casting and racism in the story also occur as part and parcel of the storyline whether acted, sung or danced. Maria and Anita's personalities exemplify a bias of what Puerto Rican women are supposed to be; Maria, the innocent virgin girl who is protected by her older brother and family and Anita, the loud vivacious loose cannon. There is no middle ground in their characters in the end, making them two dimensional. Racist and stereotypical imagery are also present in aspects of the musical's lyrics. The infamous song, "America" is always a good example.

> Puerto Rico . . .
> You ugly island. . .
> Island of tropic diseases.
> Always the hurricanes blowing,
> Always the population growing . . .
> And the money owing,
> And the babies crying,
> And the bullets flying.

> (Stephen Sondheim)

These were part of the original lyrics to "America" until "Dr. Howard Rusk, the founder of a New York medical center, complained that the song misrepresented Puerto Rico, which had, in fact, a very low instance of tropic diseases and a lower mortality rate than the continental United States" (Pollack-Pelzner). As a result, Sondheim changed the line, "Island of tropic diseases." However, the other lyrics depicting Puerto Rico as an overpopulated baby-ridden indebted violent place are shortsighted and unfortunate in such an otherwise, magnificent musical number. But stereotyping and racism in *West Side Story* are an equal opportunity presence in the Jets as they are portrayed as athletic White-trash dummies. In their "Gee, Officer Krupke" number the gang sings,

> [...] My parents treat me rough.
> With all their marijuana,
> They won't give me a puff.
> They didn't wanna have me,
> But somehow I was had.
> Leapin' lizards, that's why I'm so bad! [...]
> My Daddy beats my Mommy,
> My Mommy clobbers me,
> My Grandpa is a Commie,
> My Grandma pushes tea.
> My sister wears a mustache,
> My brother wears a dress.
> Goodness gracious, that's why I'm a mess!
>
> (Stephen Sondheim)

Alas, Sondheim explained [or confessed] to Daniel Pollack-Pelner of *The Atlantic*, "the creators were much less concerned with the sociological aspects of the story than with the theatrical ones" (Pollack-Pelzner). In fact, not only were they not concerned about the story's "sociological aspects," they were also unconcerned with a more powerful underlying aspect of the story dealing with class conflict. Both gangs are obviously from the lower classes. They fight over territory that in actuality does not belong to them. Rivals who loathe and compete with one another, they exemplify capitalist competition and are victims of the old adage, "divide and conquer."

Will this also be true of Steven Spielberg's *West Side Story* incarnation? According to screenwriter and Spielberg collaborator Tony Kushner, "Spielberg's version will turn back to the original 1957 Broadway musical by Arthur Laurents with music by Leonard Bernstein and lyrics by Steven Sondheim [...] The way I approached it and the way Steven is approaching it is using the great text [...] We started building from that" (Chi). Using the "great text" would include the typecasting and prejudice inherent in the production and storyline, not to mention the rivalry between the gangs. So, how much "building from that" will or can Kushner and Spielberg do? Rita Moreno who plays a part created for her in the Spielberg film says Spielberg is correcting "many, many of the wrongs, if not all of them" of the original musical (Fallon). Hopeful signs also come from Spielberg himself. "The story is not only a product of its time, but that time has returned, and it's returned with a kind of social fury [...] I really wanted to tell that Puerto Rican, Nuyorican experience of basically the migration to this country and the struggle to make a living, and to have children, and to battle against the obstacles of xenophobia and racial prejudice" (Breznican). All noble pursuits. If Spielberg's *West Side Story* successfully addresses the Trump neo-Nazi Proud Boys craze in this country (this is being written before Spielberg's premiere) that would be exceptional. Although, how that could happen without substantially altering the script is beyond me.

In the end, after 60 years, Puerto Ricans are still not the ones telling their *West Side Story*. White American men continue to be the ones telling *our* story, defining who *we* are and ultimately, as the "superior race" and the dominant class, colonizing us all over again. "In a feature for the *New York Times Magazine*, Sasha Weiss wondered whether this current generation of Latinx dancers 'will one day insist on staging *West Side Story* for themselves'" (Del Valle Schorske).

Works cited

Pollack-Pelzner, Daniel. "Why West Side Story Abandoned Its Queer Narrative." *The Atlantic.* 1 March 2020.

—. "Why West Side Story Abandoned Its Queer Narrative." *The Atlantic.* 1 March 2020.

Fallon, Kevin. "Rita Moreno Almost Quit Original 'West Side Story' Because It Was Racist."

The Daily Beast. 13 October 2020.

Pollack-Pelzner, Daniel. "Why West Side Story Abandoned Its Queer Narrative." *The Atlantic.* 1 March 2020.

Grady, Constance. "The new West Side Story is led by a brilliant cast. But it's reinventions don't always work." *VOX.* 11 March 2020.

Sondheim, Stephen. "America". *West Side Story.com*. https://www.westsidestory.com/america. 30 November 2020.

Pollack-Pelzner, Daniel. "Why West Side Story Abandoned Its Queer Narrative." *The Atlantic*. 1 March 2020.

Sondheim, Stephen. "Gee, Officer Krupke". *West Side Story.com*.

https://www.westsidestory.com/america. 30 November 2020.

Chi, Paul. "Steven Spielberg's West Side Story Will Go Back to Basics." *Vanity Fair*. 23 October 2018.

Fallon, Kevin. "Rita Moreno Almost Quit Original 'West Side Story' Because It Was Racist."

The Daily Beast. 13 October 2020.

Breznican, Anthony. "A First Look at Steven Spielberg's West Side Story." *Vanity Fair*. 16 March 2020.

Del Valle Schorske, Carina. "Let 'West Side Story' and Its Stereotypes Die." *New York Times*. 24 February 2020.

South Pacific,
Miss Saigon,
Soft Power and Me

Aimee Phan

In the spring of my senior year in high school, my family decided to go to Brazil. My mother was a budget traveler and loved to pull us kids out of school to take advantage of off-season deals.

Instead of agreeing to this once-in-a-lifetime vacation, I decided to stay home to participate in rehearsals for our high school's senior musical. My friends from the drama club and choir were participating, and I didn't want to miss out.

My parents asked me if I was sure about this choice, and I was pretty adamant. They warned me I'd regret it.

And I did. I do. I've never had another chance to go to Brazil. Now, whenever I revisit that adolescent decision, I think of the musical that I felt warranted such a sacrifice, *South Pacific*, and I feel nauseous.

Iconic musical kings Richard Rodgers and Oscar Hammerstein's *South Pacific* is considered one of their crown jewels. Based on a James Michener novel, *Tales of the South Pacific*, written about his experiences as a naval officer during WWII, the musical debuted in 1949 on Broadway to almost universal acclaim, gathering Tony Awards, as well as the prestigious Pulitzer Prize in drama. The show spawned a movie in 1958, and countless tours, revivals and television adaptations; its most recent Broadway revival was 2008.

People loved not only the songs, exotic locale, lowbrow humor, and swooning romances, they also lauded the show for its brave, progressive politics showcasing indigenous people, mixed-race children, and interracial romance. There are two Asian women in the main cast: Bloody Mary, and her daughter, Liat. Bloody Mary is a greedy native hustler who sells island souvenirs to American sailors—and later even offers Liat to the young, handsome, leading man, Lieutenant Joe Cable. She is a nightmare of Asian stereotypes, running around the stage shaking a shrunken head and screaming *Fo Dolla* in a heavy pidgin accent. Her daughter Liat barely speaks, except for a few broken, exquisite phrases in French. She readily goes along with her mother's scheming, seducing Joe within minutes of arriving on stage, and spends most of the musical in various arrays of tropical undress.

When Mary first presents her daughter to Joe, she identifies them both as Tonkinese, referring to Tonkin, a region in what is now northern Vietnam. In the original Broadway production, and in many versions since, non-Asian women portrayed these roles in yellowface. Juanita Hall, who originated the role of Bloody Mary on Broadway and in the film, was half-Black and half-White. Betta St. John, a White actress, originated the part of Liat on Broadway. For the film, the role was recast with France Nuyen, a half-Vietnamese and half-French actress. But if you search the internet for either of these characters, you'll find more evidence of yellowface than actual Asian actors.

For our high school production, the choir and drama teachers followed the same casting tradition, giving both parts to White girls: Bloody Mary to our choir's leading soprano, and Liat to a slender, popular girl who'd look good in skimpy island wear.

I was cast in the chorus, playing a nurse who sang and danced in the number "I'm Going to Wash That Man Right Out of My Hair." There were a handful of Asian American girls in the production, yet I don't believe any of us were really considered for these roles—even for voiceless Liat. We didn't even question it. That is how little we knew about yellowface and racism against Asians in our sheltered, privileged bubble of Orange County, California, in the 1990s. We were just happy to be part of the show.

It wasn't until I was at UCLA taking Asian American Studies classes that I began to look back at my senior musical experience with questions, then critique, then horror. The thick beige makeup both of my White classmates had to wear for yellowface. Bloody Mary's thick accent and slapstick pratfalls. The humiliating earworm of a song "Happy Talk," where Bloody Mary trills, and Liat wordlessly mimes with her hands and chest, as they enchant the gullible Joe Cable into sleeping with Liat, in order to fulfill their long game of marriage, and secure their golden ticket to the U.S.

Supposedly the musical redeems itself with the heavy-handed number "You've Got to Be Carefully Taught," sung by Joe Cable, as he blames his xenophobic family and society for forcing him to reject Liat. In its debut, the song was widely criticized for addressing the taboo of racism, for being too progressive and frank, but it doesn't hold up today either, offering too little and appearing too late in the show to inject tolerance in a musical filled with racial stereotypes and cultural assumptions.

On Facebook, I will occasionally see posts from former classmates wistfully recalling our senior musical experience. No one ever called it out for being racist or even problematic. When I private messaged a few people to discuss it, one White classmate and one Vietnamese classmate, both kind and open-minded humans, they admitted they hadn't really thought about it. Of course, they could see the problems now, but it hadn't occurred to them until I asked, because their memories of the musical experience were so pleasant. So of course, they wouldn't want to ruin it.

They were in good company. *South Pacific*'s popularity endures to this day, with a show probably playing somewhere in the country right now. While Rodgers and Hammerstein considered themselves progressive for bringing such controversial topics such as interracial relationships and mixed-race children into popular culture, they did so by amplifying some of the worst stereotypes of Asian women that exist today. The sailors may sing that Bloody Mary is "the girl I love," and that Liat is the sexy, but innocent lotus flower, but the two characters also stoke the fears many Americans harbored of the exotic war bride, a consequence of America's military interventions in Asia, when their young, promising boys returned from war with Asian wives and biracial babies.

But at least in *South Pacific*, they could correct this disturbing trend, and put these impractical lovers in their place. Of course, Joe and Liat couldn't stay together. The audience could have its tragic romance, all the while knowing such a mismatched union could never last.

American audiences adored this American soldier/Vietnamese war bride doomed fantasy so much that it appeared again, this time, with the tragedy amplified, in Alain Boublil and Claude-Michel Schönberg's musical *Miss Saigon*. After dramatizing the French Revolution in *Les Miserables*, Boublil and Schonberg selected a more recent war to romanticize: the Vietnam War.

When I was fifteen, my family traveled to New York to visit my aunt, recently arrived from Vietnam. She was the last of my father's family to immigrate to the U.S., finally doing so after multiple escape attempts after the end of the war. *Miss Saigon* was our family's first Broadway show, and we were excited. Since its London premiere in 1989, *Miss Saigon* experienced commercial worldwide success, with tours and revivals continuing today. It is Broadway's thirteenth longest running show. We'd never seen Vietnamese characters on stage before, and were hopeful, seeing how *Les Mis* glorified French rebels, casting them as complex and nuanced heroes. Perhaps this musical could offer the Vietnamese, so often stereotyped as peasants or prostitutes in Vietnam War films and television shows, the same opportunity?

We should have known better. The opening number, "The Heat is on in Saigon," almost made us leave, startling my conservative parents with the revealing bikinis and thongs of the Vietnamese sex workers on stage, gyrating against the American marine officers. The show unfolded with the same tired stereotypes of the Vietnamese people as either hookers, victims or Communist devils. It also employed yellowface in the casting of The Engineer, a half-Vietnamese half-French entrepreneur bent on, once again, pimping out a young nubile Vietnamese heroine to an American soldier.

The fairy tale was permitted to blossom past the initial lusty romance, with the sweet soldier Chris honorably impregnating the naive teenager Kim. What followed felt like another moralistic misogynistic nightmare: you can have your White man's baby, but you won't survive the end of the show. Kim manages to bring their love child to America, only to sacrifice herself with an off-screen gunshot to the heart, so that her son can be raised by Chris and his proper, White American wife, Ellen.

Afterward, I listened to the adults chat about the show. Yes, they objected to all the skin, but they also appreciated a good sob story, and how pretty Kim was, and how beautifully she sang. They did not critique the storyline, or the Vietnamese characters, or the utter lack of Asian American performers in a show that was supposed to be about their people. They were simply happy to see a story being told about their home country.

Back in Vietnam, my parents had grown up on MGM musicals that played in the theaters with Vietnamese subtitles. In America, they practiced their English by rewatching the films with my brother and me. My father loved Esther Williams, while my mother preferred Judy Garland. My dad even enrolled me in synchronized swimming classes one summer, hoping I could take after his favorite actress. These candy-colored musicals presented a golden perfect image of America to them, one I am sure persisted in the memories of many refugees migrating from Vietnam to America. So when musicals finally allowed Vietnamese people onto the stage, should they have been surprised it would reflect what Westerners already believed of them?

Like my parents, I loved musicals, yet the only characters I saw that looked like me were silent, submissive women whose only value was determined by a White man. I did not want to be Liat or Miss Saigon, which is why I was quite content playing a nurse in the senior musical, blending in with the rest of my largely White cast. I wouldn't know until much later how damaging these images were to how I saw myself, how I pursued both friendships and relationships, and how I wanted to make sure my children never struggled with seeing people who looked like them so marginalized, objectified and mistreated.

I recently watched the 1958 film version of *South Pacific* again with my own family, curious to see my children's reaction to the musical. As with most older films, my eight-year-old son and twelve-year-old daughter grew impatient with its slow start, and were confused by the dated mannerisms and ignorant jokes. They burst out laughing at the melodrama of Joe and Liat's first passionate embrace. How could the two characters kiss after saying only two sentences to each other? Why is he just dragging her around? Why is he always shirtless?

I realized then that I didn't have to intervene and make sure they weren't hurt or ashamed by Bloody Mary and Liat's cartoonish behavior, like I had been. Despite sharing the same racial heritage, they wisely understood they were nothing like these people.

When they are old enough, I'd love to take them to see *Soft Power*, the David Henry Hwang musical which played in San Francisco in 2018. A satire inspired by *The King and I*, yet another Rodgers and Hammerstein tale set in Southeast Asia, *Soft Power* follows a Chinese theater producer venturing into the Wild West of America, and encountering exotic, mysterious aspects of the U.S., such as a fancy McDonald's restaurant, good guys with guns, Hilary Clinton as Wonder Woman, and the absurdity of the electoral college. The largely Asian American cast take on playfully inaccurate regional accents while performing in whiteface. The choices in the show feel satisfying, smart and scathing. It was our musical revenge against every song, dance and inaccuracy we'd seen in the past. If any critic argued that the White stereotypes went too far, you'd only have to point back at any of Broadway musicals' depictions of people of color, particularly Asians, in response.

The theater was not at capacity during the evening show, perhaps a harbinger of the show's short-lived and (so far) final run in New York. But it was full of warmth and laughter that summer evening, as we laughed and commiserated with the jokes we'd never before heard on stage. *Soft Power* only lasted two months Off Broadway in 2019, but I hope it will have the opportunity to come back. There is an audience waiting for it. There is room for it, and more.

When You Mess with Creation Myths, the Knives Come Out*

Ishmael Reed

I would have ended my challenge to *Hamilton, The Revolution* after a four-night reading of the script that took place at the Nuyorican Poets Café last January. It was one of the actors, Robert Mailer Anderson, a filmmaker (*Windows on the World*) and novelist, who said that he'd put up money for a full production. He doubled the amount that he promised. The second largest contributors were the late Toni Morrison and her son, Ford, who saved us big bucks by making their New York apartment available to us during rehearsals and performances. Plus audience members sent us donations. But even with the reading, which cost me $5,000.00, the backlash from "Hamilfans" was furious.

First, they insisted that I had no right to write a play about a musical that I hadn't seen, even

First published online by *Counterpunch*, September 13, 2019.

though I had read Lin-Manuel Miranda's book for *Hamilton, The Revolution* many times, and also quoted from Miranda's play in my script. So I saw it. I revised my script based upon what I'd witnessed and wrote about my experience in *The San Francisco Chronicle*[1] and spoke about it when interviewed on HBO's *Vice News*.[2] I've kept revising. For example, I added some lines about the historian Ron Chernow's speech at the 2019 White House Correspondents' Dinner, which he ended by condemning slavery after spending the first minutes honoring slave owners.

Lin-Manuel Miranda says he based his musical on Chernow's book. Yet, those who criticized me for not having seen *Hamilton, The Revolution* are among those who have criticized my play without having seen it. The ad hominem attacks in the comments section of *The Times* merely reflected the damage that an emphasis on European studies has done to American intellectuals.

Having visited Europe many times since my first trip at the age of 17, I can say that they don't even get Europe right. These brightest and best, who responded to the January 2019 reading and the following May-June production of my play, know very little about American History and depend upon imports to influence their intellectual grounding. For a project, I examined *The Village Voice*'s cultural coverage for the summer of 1985. You couldn't help but notice the popularity of

French films and literature. Jean-Paul Sartre and Jean Genet were big. William Barrett, the author of *The Truants*,[3] writes about how the '50s New York Intelligentsia eagerly awaited French intellectuals to arrive in New York to give them guidance.

One refreshing item about Miranda's *Hamilton* is that it does include American characters. I agree with my critics, the Hamilfans, that Miranda has the right to take liberties with their histories, but in doing so, he covered up their crimes. Some of those who should know better have endorsed this billion-dollar entertainment. President Obama aided the production by recording George Washington's Farewell Address with a Black choir humming softly in the background. George Washington raffled off slave children to pay his debts.[4]

When I saw Black students who were *Hamilton* fans, pose with Lin-Manuel Miranda, I was wondering whether they knew that in 1793 Hamilton's in-laws, the Schuylers, agitated for the hanging of three Black Albany teenagers based on trumped-up charges. Random House will publish my poem about the incident.

Because I have cred with the Black media, I haven't been dependent upon acceptance from mainstream critics. My play, *The Final Version*, (2013) saw successful attendance even though temperatures were so cold that some performances were canceled. It was the Black media and word of mouth that filled the seats at the Nuyorican Poets Café. And so

I wasn't surprised that *The Times* printed a hit piece. *Hamilton* has been good for their revenue stream. It was written by a critic who came to the United States from Europe in the 1980s. She objected to the way that the play treated Miranda and Ron Chernow, whom she referred to as "Ron." Most of the performances earned standing ovations and packed houses. The audience response was often raucous as audience members shouted their approval or disapproval with the actors' lines. *The Times* critic, however, said that she didn't find the play "engaging." For Black playwrights of the 1950s and '60s a negative review from *The Times* would have been career-ending. James Baldwin became distraught after such reviews of his play, *Blues for Mr. Charlie*. They ended Amiri Baraka's career with *Dutchman*, even though he continued to write brilliant plays. According to a recent *Times*' article, some Black playwrights still sweat the response from mainstream critics. This situation has changed with the advent of online sites like *CounterPunch* and social media, where writers can appeal to broad audiences directly. Another hit came from NPR's *Wait, Wait Don't Tell Me*, whose panelists spent five minutes or so ridiculing my script and me without having read the script. I've sent three letters to NPR asking for a chance to reply only to get the runaround. NPR is now involved in a heated controversy as the Black and Hispanic staff have signed a letter objecting to remarks made by the new director.[5]

The Nation assigned a Harvard undergraduate to review the play. I could tell that she hadn't seen the play, and based her review on an early version of the script that they requested. She ended the review by implying that Amiri Baraka could have written a better play. She's not aware that she was invoking the old Pat Juber, which is the slavery term for pitting one Black person against the other for the entertainment of White onlookers. Pat Juber has been a form of entertainment for the Manhattan intellectual elite dating back to before the 1920s. I appreciate Baraka's work so much that I published two of his books and an excerpt from his unpublished novel in my magazine *Konch*, when nobody else would publish them. The editors at *The Nation* invited me to engage in a back and forth with this student. No. I asked her to have an exchange with me at my magazine *Konch,* at ishmaelreedpub.com. So far, no response. When *The Nation* published a poem that indicted the homeless as chiselers, I responded with a poem that indicted the banks as the real chiselers. It was rejected.

The high point of the June run occurred when the nine-year-old grandson of Diana Ross said, during the question-and-answer period, thank you for acquainting me with American history. He introduced the performance that night by reading a poem written by Langston Hughes. I want more students to see my play so that they can hear the comments of slaves, Native Americans, and indentured servants about the Hamilton and Schuyler families. My characters don't humiliate Lin-Manuel Miranda as Hamilfans have charged. They educate him!! We have all been victims of an Anglo-centered curriculum.

I've written to the Gilder Lehrman Institute of American History, which bought 22,000 tickets for students to see *Hamilton*, to purchase tickets for students to see *The Haunting of Lin-Manuel Miranda*. PowerHouse Books is going to publish my script so that it will be available to some students. Random House will distribute them. [Archway, an imprint of PowerHouse Books, published the play in Fall, 2020.] A Puerto Rican group is interested in mounting a performance there. A group in Toronto wants to do the play next year to coincide with the opening of the *Hamilton* bonanza in Toronto.

Because of our efforts, the *Hamilton* people have had to retreat from their portrayal of Hamilton as an "abolitionist." In their failed Chicago exhibit, their marketing line became that he was opposed to slavery.[6] Opposed to slavery? When the 1791 revolt in Haiti occurred, Hamilton sided with the French slaveholders.[7] The new line was featured in the Chicago exhibit "Hamilton" which had to close. We're running for another month. From the first week in October to the final week. Details at Nuyorican.org. I'm putting up thousands of my dollars because for me this has become a mission. We cannot challenge the new lies unless we contest the old ones. Some contributions have come through from GoFundMe. Unlike their "Hamilton," we don't have support from the Rockefellers. Our support has come from those whom Hamilton called the rabble. We rabble have to put Broadway on notice that they can no longer sugarcoat the careers of slave masters and genocidal maniacs like Andrew Jackson without a vigorous challenge.

Responding to *Bloody Bloody Andrew Jackson* & Claiming the Power of Native Voice

Betsy Theobald Richards
(Cherokee Nation)

> "*The great enemy of truth is very often not the lie—deliberate, contrived and dishonest—but the myth—persistent—persuasive and unrealistic. Too often we hold fast to the clichés of our forebears. We subject all facts to a prefabricated set of interpretations. We enjoy the comfort of opinion without the discomfort of thought.*" John F. Kennedy

After decades of fighting erasure from our stages and screens, I was delighted this past month, when it was announced that Lakota playwright Larissa FastHorse won the 2020 MacArthur "Genius" Award for her phenomenal body of work, dramatizing contemporary Native lives while simultaneously translating for, and critiquing, mainstream audiences. This highly visible award was not only a win for diversity at a time when the country is in the midst of a national reckoning on race, history, and justice. More importantly, it was a triumph of something all of us in the Indigenous community care about—having our voices, perspectives, and visions not only heard, but upheld in our national narrative.

Despite Ms. FastHorse and other Native artists' recent noteworthy honors (Cheyenne/Arapaho author Tommy Orange's National Book Award, Muskogee writer Joy Harjo's reappointment as U.S. Poet Laureate, among others), these moments of national recognition are too few and far between. As the 2018-released public-opinion research report *Reclaiming Native Truth* rigorously affirmed, "contemporary Native Americans are, for the most part, invisible in the United States. Most Americans know little about Native history or our present day lives and are guided by myths and romanticized stereotypes.... we now have documented evidence of how those biases are holding back Native Americans from political, economic and social equity as well as respectful representation."

"Invisibility of Native peoples to most of America threatens our fundamental rights and the well being of our children," says Crystal Echo Hawk (Pawnee), President of IllumiNative, an organization dedicated to narrative change for Native Americans. "We are invisible within government, Hollywood, the news media, and in our schools.... Our invisibility and erasure are seen as normal." This narrative removal plays out with our well-meaning allies, as well as our opponents, and most often leaves Native artists swimming in not-so-receptive cultural waters.

Ms. FastHorse's honor is particularly poignant to me, because it was almost exactly 10 years ago that I found myself stepping down in protest from my role as Native Theater Initiative Fellow at the New York Shakespeare Festival's Public Theater, a prominent Off-Broadway venue, when they moved their hit emo-rock musical *Bloody, Bloody Andrew Jackson* to Broadway despite vehement protests from the Native community. *The New York Times* theater critic Ben Brantley was calling it "the most entertaining and most perceptive political theater of the season," and it was playing to record sold out houses, extended three times, and became the second highest-grossing show in the downtown institution's history.

A precursor to their 2015 mega-founding fathers-hit *Hamilton,* 2010's *Bloody Bloody Andrew Jackson was* created, produced and acted by an all-White team including writer/director Alex Timbers, Artistic Director of the award-winning, experimental theater company Les Freres Corbusier and the late composer/lyricist Michael Friedman, founding Artist Associate of The Civilians. As described by D. M. Levine in Politico, the musical "is a farce meant to draw comic parallels between Jackson's populism and some of the folksy populism peddled by politicians in our modern era. It does this, at least in part, by poking relentless fun at Jackson's friends, enemies and victims (Henry Clay, John Quincy Adams and John C. Calhoun, for example, are all portrayed as effeminate idiots)—and this includes Native Americans." The Public was marketing this hip, "historical" piece to school groups, was selling "Andrew Jackson is a Rockstar" buttons, and, for the first time, was allowing alcohol to be taken into the building's Newman Theater. It was a raucous and sexy social critique on the 21st century Tea Party, starring tight-panted Benjamin Walker in eyeliner and celebrating, as *The New York Times*' Brantley put it "Jackson's road from a backwoods boyhood to his fraught tenures as a land-snatching, Indian-slaughtering general and president."

As a citizen of the Cherokee Nation (whose ancestors were forced to walk the Trail of Tears by Andrew Jackson), theater artist, and former Ford Foundation Native arts funder (whose portfolio was the key supporter of the Native Theater Initiative), I was open to possibilities when Artistic Director Oskar Eustis brought me, excitedly, as the Native Initiative Fellow to the dress rehearsal for something he described to me as a critique of Andrew Jackson. New York Shakespeare Festival/Public Theater Associate Producer Mandy Hackett, primed me for the evening ahead, saying that it brilliantly poked fun at everyone, "just like *The Daily Show*."

In the darkened theater that night, I sat there, aghast, next to Mr. Eustis, my long-time Native theater ally and collaborator (we had worked together to produce two Native theater festivals and a few productions when he was Artistic Director of Trinity Rep and I was working for the Mashantucket Pequot Tribal Nation's museum). My heart was pounding, and my stomach turned, as I witnessed White actors in ridiculous redface, perform a humorous song about ten ways to kill Indians, and Native chiefs such as the great Sauk tribal leader Black Hawk, falsely portrayed as turncoats and sellouts. It was all met with uproarious laughter and applause from the rest of the audience.

Even more frightening was the fact that a good deal of the dramatic action in this raucous political circus was driven by a historically inaccurate and culturally biased plot point that as Andrew Jackson biographer Jon Meacham pointed out in *The New York Times*, "gives Jackson something of a fictional out on the [Trail of Tears] issue." At the beginning of the show is a vignette of Jackson's parents being murdered by comic Native "sniper" arrows. Even Meacham critiques that this was "implying that his parents were murdered by Indians and thus casting the ensuing decades of conquest and deceit as a revenge drama. Never happened."

As former Amerinda Theater Artistic Director and Native Theater Initiative Advisor Steve Elm (Oneida) put it, *Bloody, Bloody Andrew Jackson* "seemed to be expressly written without any idea that there are still Native people alive," or in other words, the false history portrayed Native genocide as successful and implied that the dominant culture's imagined historic "savages" are complicit in their own suffering. Donning redface to both embody and erase Native people is as American as apple pie (e.g., the Boston Tea Party), and as Dakota author and scholar Philip Deloria suggests in his book *Playing Indian* has "helped generations of White Americans define, mask, and evade paradoxes stemming from simultaneous construction and destruction of these Native peoples."

That night during dress rehearsal, I couldn't fathom how this, the people's theater, that I held so close to my heart (I had worked for the Public on the house staff as an undergrad at NYU during Joseph Papp's tenure in the early '80s and done readings of Native plays and co-produced a show under JoAnne Akalaitis' leadership) could be simultaneously supporting Native writers like William S. Yellow Robe (Assiniboine), Rhiana Yazzie (Navajo), Darrell Dennis (Shuswap), and Joy Harjo (Muskogee Creek) while producing this "he's sexy, naughty, and ... it's complicated" portrayal of slave owner and Indian-killer-in-Chief Andrew Jackson.

I had a few difficult meetings with the leadership and a lunch with Mr. Timbers and Mr. Friedman, filled with the emotional and mental labor of repeatedly trying to explain how not only was this hit show incredibly offensive to Native people, but more importantly, its historical fabrications actually underscored false beliefs and attitudes that contribute to Native peoples being at the bottom of social and economic indicators in the United States. After our conversations, and as the show started its run downtown, Mr. Eustis reached out to the wider Native theater community to express regret and build bridges, all framed around dialogue and protection of Timbers' and Friedman's artistic freedom of expression. The Public's artistic leadership gave many members of the Indigenous community comps to the show. Some Native people that attended booed and others wrote furious letters to the Public's management. Danielle Soames (Mohawk) co-founder of Mixed Phoenix Theater Group told *Politico*'s D.M. Levine "there's a Native Theater Initiative – they have some sense of responsibility by having this Initiative and yet they're not honoring that Initiative by producing a show like this."

A series of one-on-one listening sessions led to a major meeting at the end of the Off-Broadway run, attended by leading members of the NYC Native theater community including Muriel Miguel (Kuna/Rappahannock) of Spiderwoman Theater, Steve Elm (Oneida), James Fall (Stockbridge/Munsee), Vickie Ramirez (Tuscarora), Murielle Borst-Tarrant (Kuna/Rappahannock) and many others, both locally and from across the country. Since any script changes during the downtown run were off the table, Mr. Eustis expressed interest in finding easy fixes for the Broadway run "that wouldn't in any way have changed what the play was doing, that wouldn't remotely have been censoring Alex and Michael but would have been appropriate gestures." (*Politico*)

Bloody Bloody Andrew Jackson transferred to the Bernard B. Jacobs Theatre on Broadway on September 20, 2010, under the advertising slogan "History Just Got Sexypants!" The creative team and producers also clung to the dramatically efficient portrayal of Jackson's Indian removal and genocide as revenge for his parents' fictional murder by Native Americans, despite all the requests, protests by, and dialogue with the Native community. Out of the listening sessions, the producers did change the name of the great Sauk tribal leader BlackHawk to a fictionalized Black Fox. It was not a commercial success and closed on January 2, 2011, after 120 performances.

This was a painful, yet watershed moment for me and really brought to light how powerful dominant narratives, or stories told in service of the dominant social group's interests and ideologies "are so normalized through their repetition and authority, they have the illusion of being objective and apolitical, when in fact they are neither" (University of Michigan/Inclusive Teaching Guide).

In fact, my intention here is not to resurrect damage done by *Bloody Bloody Andrew Jackson* but to lift up how tasty and easily digested these myths (the ones that justify dominance and support status quo) are within theaters that create spaces dedicated to risk-taking, diverse voices, and freedom of expression.

Most importantly, I'd like to underscore how some of the most important work ahead for Native American and other BIPOC artists (and their allies) is using stories for culture change that intentionally seek to shift beliefs, perceptions and behaviors towards a more equitable society, not merely an effort for more diverse representation. As National Medal of Freedom-awardee Hodulgee Muskogee writer and advocate Suzan Harjo says "we carry cultural wisdom and professional expertise into every sector of society, both in our tribes and in American communities. We are artists, history makers and storytellers, adept at sharing our past and our current reality. This must become the narrative, replacing the erasure that obscures our true identities and sanctions their replacement with false personae." (*Reclaiming Native Truth*).

Ten years on, the good news is that, despite the consistent strong pull of myth and misinformation, *Reclaiming Native Truth*'s public opinion polling has found that 78 percent of Americans are now open to learning more about Native Americans. This hunger for a new narrative framework is a hopeful trend for a new generation of Native play-wrights like Larissa FastHorse and her contemporaries such as Mary Kathryn Nagle (Cherokee Nation), Ty Defoe (Ojibwe/Oneida), Tara Moses (Seminole Nation of Oklahoma), and Vera Starbard (Tlingit/Dena'ina). And newsflash: After I stepped down from my role at The Public, I have continued to at times serve as a director/dramaturg, but that experience propelled me to commit much of the last decade working for narrative change at The Opportunity Agenda, partnering with a powerful and diverse network of artists to support them in telling compelling stories that will change the national conversation and shift culture.

If you'd like to join me in celebrating voice, artistry, and storytelling from a Native perspective, and helping to shift harmful narratives, you can take action by (1) supporting Native-led Theater companies located across the United States from Safe Harbors Indigenous Collective and The American Indian Community House in New York, New Native Theater in the Twin Cities, and Native Voices at the Autrey in Los Angeles, among others; and (2) learning more about being an ally for Native narrative change from IllumiNative (IllumiNatives.org). Together, we can end erasure, celebrate the voice and visions of Native storytellers, and create a culture where we see and hear each other's past, present, and future.

Dance and Song Before Story: Was *Flower Drum Song* a Phantasy?

Shawn Wong interviewed by Ishmael Reed

Ishmael Reed: I'm looking at C.Y. (Chin Yang) Lee. I just saw the film version of *Flower Drum Song*, which was awful, which was terrible.

Shawn Wong: It had a lot of company in the early sixties, you know.

Ishmael Reed: What do you mean by that?

Shawn Wong: There were a lot of movies like that. *My Geisha*, and then there was *Love is a Many-Splendored Thing* and *The World of Suzie Wong*. They all came out within a few years of each other. William Holden was always saving some Chinese girl or Marlon Brando saving some Japanese girl, so *Flower Drum Song*, [Broadway premiere, 1958; film released in 1961], was in good company at that time. I think the reason for that was restrictive immigration laws. Asians were no longer an immigration threat and so portrayals became sort of positive stereotypes. We just sing and dance in the streets of Chinatown and we don't cause any trouble like those Black people who are demonstrating for Civil Rights and stuff.

Ishmael Reed: Even for White theater, this musical seemed to be heavily propagandistic towards patriotism. There were even these sort of patriotic bands marching in Chinatown, and flags everywhere.

Shawn Wong: I think it was to show Chinese Americans as the opposite of Communist Chinese. Communism was rising in China. So to portray the Chinese in America as on the side of the Taiwan nationalists and not on the side of the Red Chinese was a safe bet.

Ishmael Reed: So they were saying, "We are people, too. Loyal Americans like the rest of you." That's what seemed to be the message.

Shawn Wong: Yeah, and we were no threat because *Flower Drum Song* was self-contained within Chinatown. We weren't out there marching in the streets. We had our own problems, you know.

Ishmael Reed: Yeah, and you weren't going out into the suburbs threatening White women.

Shawn Wong: That's right. We weren't out there like you people marching and stuff, and so in 1961 when the movie came out, that was the first time "Model Minority" was ever mentioned.

Ishmael Reed: Is that right?

Shawn Wong: It was mentioned in *U.S. News and World Report* and in 1961 it was when the term "Model Minority" was linked to Asian people.

Ishmael Reed: Yeah, lumping them altogether.

Shawn Wong: So when you look at *Flower Drum Song*, it's the Model Minority. "Aren't they cute? They're no threat," and the unspoken message is, "Why can't you Black people be loyal Americans like the Asians, the Model Minority?"

Ishmael Reed: I noticed in the choreography, as I pointed out to Carla [Blank], that it seemed like a copy of *An American in Paris* with Gene Kelly. Then I found Gene Kelly had a role in the musical on Broadway.

Shawn Wong: I didn't know that.

Ishmael Reed: He was hired to be the stage director and a lot of the dance choreography was like duplicative of the kind of stuff you got on Broadway. You can also say there was non-traditional casting, but for the wrong reasons, right? They just hired some of the Chinese Americans and there's a Black woman, Juanita Hall, who plays the sister-in-law of Wang Chi Yang (Benson Fong), and they just seemed to have done some lazy casting.

Shawn Wong: They continued to put actors in Yellow Face. In the movie Juanita Hall was playing the Chinese woman's role that she created on Broadway. On the other hand, I think I was twelve when the movie came out, but I also remember at that age going, "Wow. I've never seen Chinese people in the movies before that weren't killers and soldiers and martial artists and Asian villains." I think as a kid my first reaction was, "Wow, at least some of them are speaking without an accent."

Ishmael Reed: Well, what was the reaction of your folks and people in your community when *Flower Drum Song* came out?

Shawn Wong: At the time it was interesting because it was positive, because there was not a portrayal like that anywhere on the silver screen before that. It was so stereotyped but at least we were being talented. We were singing and dancing and speaking English without an accent. It was completely racist, but at the same time I think a lot of Chinese Americans celebrated it. It did portray a real moment in history, which was the Chinese nightclubs. Because Chinese couldn't go to the White nightclubs, they started their own nightclubs.

Ishmael Reed: I thought it was like the Cotton Club.

Shawn Wong: Same idea as Harlem. In those days there was a big nightclub scene and so

Chinatown started their own nightclubs and so the musical does mimic the real-life portrayal of those nightclubs.

Ishmael Reed: But in the film version you see wealthy White people coming in there.

Shawn Wong: Right, which is probably the same thing that happened in Harlem. It became cool for the White people to go into the ghetto and in this case lust after and worship Asian women, but not so much the men. The men don't come off very well in *Flower Drum Song*.

Ishmael Reed: I want to jump forward to David Henry Hwang and this thing he did called *Soft Power*. Are you acquainted with that musical? (Premiere Los Angeles, 2018; NYC's Public Theater production, 2019)

Shawn Wong: No, I'm not.

Ishmael Reed: He seems to be trailing the ghosts of Rodgers and Hammerstein. He seems to recycle some of their stuff. It's about a Chinese American playwright who is asked to do a rewrite of *The King and I*. He did a plot rewrite of *Flower Drum Song* also (Broadway premiere, 2002) and kept some of the racist songs except for "Chop Suey," which was awful, but now he's done this thing called *Soft Power* where it preaches the same thing of assimilation and I wonder has he ever been to China.

Shawn Wong: I don't know. Can't answer that.

Ishmael Reed: This *Soft Power* opens with the same thing as *Flower Drum Song*, where a traditional father salutes his daughter for being dutiful like a traditional Chinese daughter. The women that we met in China were not dutiful. They were like the avant-garde and very hip, so I was just wondering if he had ever gone there.

Shawn Wong: I don't know. He probably has.

Ishmael Reed: But he recycles the whole thing about assimilation being good.

Shawn Wong: He's probably only been to China since he's been famous.

Ishmael Reed: Was he stabbed?

Shawn Wong: Yeah, he was. He was mugged and stabbed on the streets of New York.

Ishmael Reed: Well this *Soft Power* is about an Asian American playwright who's stabbed.

Shawn Wong: Yeah, that would be him.

Ishmael Reed: So I am just wondering, what is this thing about him and Rodgers and Hammerstein.

Shawn Wong: I don't know. It's sort of like back in the seventies when they wanted to remake *Charlie Chan* and they wanted a Chinese American to rewrite *Charlie Chan*. It's a no-win situation being asked to recreate a racist image.

Ishmael Reed: The writer of the novel that *Flower Drum Song* is adapted from, C.Y. Lee, went to Yale. Do you think that's where he was suckered into something called the American Dream? I mean that was originally a Christian school whose goal was to create young Christian gentlemen.

Shawn Wong: I don't know if it's the American Dream, as C.Y. Lee was from China. He's from mainland China, super educated, came over to the United States, was an accomplished writer, but very much embraced the sort of White Christian POV. Again, in order to be accepted you had to sort of embrace the Christianity. It's sort of the consequence of the Missionary Movement in China. If you prove you're a Christian, then you're the good kind of immigrant.

Ishmael Reed: It seems some of the tragedies that occur in the novel were taken out. For example, there is a scene in the movie where the dressmaker Helen Chao (Reiko Sato) has a crush on the son. There was a choreographed number where this character was surrounded by all of these guys. It just seemed not to belong there and then I find in the novel she commits suicide. I was just wondering did they only keep the happy parts?

Shawn Wong: Yeah, yeah, absolutely. It's a musical. The only Asian women who die, die to benefit White men.

Ishmael Reed: You got to go into that.

Shawn Wong: Like *Madame Butterfly* and *Miss Saigon*. The Asian woman dies to make the White man's life a little easier. That Madame Butterfly trope has been reintroduced over and over and over again, so that in a movie like *Flower Drum Song*, there's no benefit for an Asian woman committing suicide since the White man isn't benefiting from it.

Ishmael Reed: It also removes the dark element of Lee's work, including Helen Chao's suicide after her desperate fling with Todd. They added the festive club night spot and emphasized romantic elements of the story.

Shawn Wong: It's a musical.

Ishmael Reed: Alice Walker said Stephen Spielberg's film version of her novel was not based on her novel. She was very upset. What happens to these ethnic materials in the hands of White men? This seems like a regular practice. They seem to be transformed, like in Rodgers and Hammerstein. I mean the lyrics are terrible, awful. I read where David Henry Hwang had to please investors. Is that what happens?

Shawn Wong: Oh, I'm sure. That's required some big-time investment, probably. You get caught in that trap. Pay to play.

Ishmael Reed: They wanted Yul Brynner as director originally.

Shawn Wong: Is that because of *The King and I*?

Ishmael Reed: That's right. Because of the 1951 *The King and I*. So these White guys take it over. They take it on, and it becomes different from the original text.

Shawn Wong: Well, yeah. That's happened over and over.

Ishmael Reed: Carla [Blank] asked if David Henry Hwang was the go-to Chinese writer now? How many scripts by Chinese American writers have to be sacrificed so they can have one Model Minority to talk about?

Carla Blank: This is Broadway we're talking about.

Shawn Wong: I would say David is the… there's always just room for one.

Ishmael Reed: He's palatable, right? He's compatible with their aims, right?

Shawn Wong: He's like Black screen writers. In a writer's room there's room for one. We got one in our writer's room, but there's never two.

Ishmael Reed: Later on there was a backlash on *Flower Drum Song* and I think you guys [Frank Chin, Jeffery Paul Chan, Lawson Fusao Inada, and Shawn Wong, the co-editors of the anthology

Aiiieeeee!] lead to the reaction to it. Why do you think that happened?

Shawn Wong: I think it's partly due to the fact that in *Aiiieeeee!* we were talking about there being two kinds of racism: racist hate and racist love. In *Flower Drum Song* there was an example of racist love. It's still racist, but it's racist in a positive light. Just like Stepin Fetchit. It's endearing but ultimately an extremely racist character, just like Hop Sing in *Bonanza*. White women could walk though his kitchen on Ponderosa Ranch and know that they're not going to be accosted or assaulted.

Ishmael Reed: [*To Carla Blank*] Did you have any questions?

Carla Blank: Why can they claim that there was something traditional about it?

Ishmael Reed: There was not a single scene belonging to traditional Chinese dance in that musical. They were saying they had made a compromise saying that it was fifty percent traditional. Weren't they trying to say they struck a middle ground culturally? That it's fifty percent Chinese traditional and fifty percent American? It seems like ninety-nine percent of it was accepting American values.

Shawn Wong: I think the real Chinatown nightclubs were trying to emulate American nightclubs. They had an Asian theme, a Chinese theme, but they were trying to be the typical midtown kind of nightclub that was popular at that time. So the kind of musical productions that were put on there might be Asian customs and slightly Asianized music, but it was ultimately always Western. That's what audiences wanted.

Ishmael Reed: The younger brother (Wang San, played by Patrick Adiarte) who goes around in these baseball outfits and everything and poses as Paul Revere in a parade or something indicates the third generation will be completely American.

Shawn Wong: Yeah, and that also is no threat, the idea that we'll be completely assimilated.

Ishmael Reed: Has that happened?

Shawn Wong: It's hard to say because the majority of Asians in the United States are foreign born. People like me who are American-born Asians are in the minority. We're the exception rather than the rule.

Ishmael Reed: How are you treated by the immigrants?

Shawn Wong: Of course, the Asian population has changed drastically from when *Flower Drum Song* came out. Back in those days there were just three Asian groups: Filipinos, Japanese and Chinese, because of restrictive immigration laws. Then later in the mid-sixties and mid-seventies the Asian population in America and its demographics began to change drastically and so lots of recent immigrants don't like the term "Asian American" because it doesn't describe who they are. They don't understand it's a political term. "I'm not Asian American. I'm Cambodian." "I'm Vietnamese."

Ishmael Reed: We get that from the Africans. "I'm Nigerian." "I'm Ghanaian." Let me ask you about Linda Low, Sammy Fong's girlfriend.

Shawn Wong: That's Nancy Kwan's character. It made her a superstar.

Ishmael Reed: She got more movie roles?

Shawn Wong: To play similar kinds of things. In that case, the attractive Asian woman who's attracted to White men. You see her in movies with William Holden and the leading men of the day.

Ishmael Reed: And Mei Li. Too good to be true?

Shawn Wong: Way too good to be true.

Ishmael Reed: This saintly girl.

Carla Blank: She was played by a Japanese actress, Miyoshi Umeki.

Ishmael Reed: She's Japanese?

Shawn Wong: Yeah, she's Japanese. You see her character played in movies over and over and over.

Ishmael Reed: Who are some of the male actors in that movie who got repeated roles?

Shawn Wong: I guess Jimmy Shigeta was in it, was he?

Carla Blank: He plays Wang Ta, the good son.

Ishmael Reed: What about Keye Luke?

Shawn Wong: He made his mark as Charlie Chan's number one son.

Ishmael Reed: Miyoshi Umeki played in Marlon Brando's *Sayonara*. She got an Oscar.

Shawn Wong: Yeah, she played the same character over and over and over. Shy, docile, obedient. Wasn't she also in *The Courtship of Eddie's Father* as the housekeeper? I believe she was and then James Shigeta was the first Asian actor to kiss a White woman in a movie and not be killed by the end of the movie. I think it was called *The Crimson Kimono*. He plays an L.A. detective, and he falls in love with a White woman, and they kiss and he didn't die.

Ishmael Reed: Well David Henry Hwang has a Chinese guy in a romance with a White woman in this *Soft Power* thing that he did. As a matter of fact, I think there are more White people in the cast than Asian Americans.

Shawn Wong: Somebody probably told them what the number had to be.

Ishmael Reed: And how to attract an audience. The Chinese Americans were the first ones to protest Stephen Spielberg for his *Indiana Jones*. They accused him of having White men saving minority women from the minority men. Okay we have a movie from the 1980s that is considered a classic. Is there an independent Asian American film movement that combats this stuff out of Broadway and Hollywood? Talk about your film, *Americanese*.

Shawn Wong: The film version of my novel, the example I use is the movie, *Crash*. The message in that movie is really simple. Racism is bad and it never goes beyond that definition. That's all it is. Racism is bad and if you didn't know it was bad, there's that scene where the car's overturned. Matt Dillon crawls into the car and meets the Black woman he assaulted and molested and she'd rather die in a burning car than have him touch her again. So if you didn't know racism was bad, that was the scene that convinced you that racism was bad. Then in my movie *Americanese* we decided that the message had to be so much more complex about racism and so much more about nuance, that it's not good or bad, it can occur in your own family or in your own relationship and how you negotiate that territory by bringing that out in the open or for many of us you choose silence in order to preserve whatever that relationship is, whether it's the parent or child or...

Ishmael Reed: So what are you doing with it?

Shawn Wong: The producer wants to recut the movie and then put it on streaming.

Ishmael Reed: That's a good idea.

Shawn Wong: We had an actor in there, Sab Shimono, who was an actor for forty years and he was playing the father, and during the filming he came up to me and said, "In forty years this was the first role here I was able to cry and tell a joke in the same movie." Actor and director Joan Chin, who plays the lead, she agreed to be in the movie at minimum wage because even for her, she makes her own movies, she goes, "The opportunity to play a character this complex does not come along." That was the idea. In a movie like *Crash* none of the characters are complex.

Ishmael Reed: They made the cop the hero, and he passes on his bad habits to a younger generation of policemen—that you can plant evidence and cover it up. So things have not changed since *Flower Drum Song,* generally. Is that what you're saying? David Hwang has not pushed the curve further, or the other playwrights?

Shawn Wong: I would say the only thing that has changed is that there are so many more Asian Americans filmmakers now and that they make their own movies. I would say that roles for Asian American actors are still somewhat limited.

Ishmael Reed: I talked to the filmmaker, Robert Polidori, who shot my film, *Personal Problems*, and he said that equipment is so cheap nowadays that there's really no excuse for people not making their own films.

Shawn Wong: You don't need 35mm film anymore. My movie was one of the last movies made in 35mm. On the big screen the color is gorgeous, but yeah, you're right. Not only can you film everything on digital, but you can have several cameras going at once and make the movie in half the time.

Ishmael Reed: Why do you think there's reluctance to take advantage of this?

Shawn Wong: I think independent filmmakers are taking advantage of it. When you take a look at the Asian American film festivals around the country, there's a huge variety of films. That is encouraging to see, and I think part of it's like you said, the cost is way down.

Carla Blank: What about live theater?

Ishmael Reed: What about live theater? I know the Asian American Theater closed down in San Francisco.

Shawn Wong: There are still very few, like East/West players in L.A., and probably small groups here and there.

Carla Blank: There is still the Asian American Performers Action Coalition.

Ishmael Reed: Is Broadway hopeless?

Shawn Wong: Look at what Broadway does. Forget about the minorities. They don't have any writers. All they do is reprisals of old musicals.

Carla Blank: And Disney.

Ishmael Reed: And Disney. What about Disney?

Shawn Wong: And Disney. If you had writers… like some of the best films out there are Pixar films. *Toy Story* and stuff. Those are some great stories, like *Up* and stuff like that. But the problem with Broadway is the least amount of money is spent on the most important part, which is the story.

Ishmael Reed: Yeah, I think you're right about that. Like Lin-Manuel Miranda. I think he was going for show tunes and big production numbers and not really worrying about the story.

Shawn Wong: You got the least amount of money spent on the most important part. So you get these thin story lines. It's a successful show, but look how thin the lines are in *Miss Saigon*. They can't even think of an original plot.

Ishmael Reed: The one I saw had a Black pimp. That's our role. Let me ask you a question that I wanted to ask you in the beginning. Rodgers and Hammerstein were members of a persecuted minority. Do you think that since assimilation worked for them, they were recommending it to others, and that's how we got *Flower Drum Song*?

Shawn Wong: I don't think *Flower Drum Song* was recommending assimilation. It had already happened because of institutionalized racism and racist immigration laws. The population of Chinese Americans in the 1950s was at an all-time low. There were no families like how they appeared in that show. For a while, Chinese women were not allowed to enter the United States. What you saw on stage was an aberration. There weren't any Chinese American kids and fully formed families so to speak. What was being depicted was not in fact a reality and we posed no threat in terms of numbers. It always comes down to numbers.

Ishmael Reed: Shawn, thanks for this.

Shawn Wong: Sure. Good to talk to you. Take it easy.

Ishmael Reed: Bye.

Oklahoma!: As American as Apple Pie and Broken Treaties*

David Yearsley

While White Supremacists were staging a Nuremberg-style Nazi torchlight parade down in Dixie last Friday night I joined an almost exclusively White audience on the verdant shores of Otsego Lake just north of Cooperstown, New York, at the Glimmerglass Opera House for a staged entertainment about American ethnic cleansing, one so effective in its procedures that all the ethnics had indeed been scrubbed from the story, if not from the cast. With its feast of winning songs and swirling dances crowned by a jury-tampering frontier-justice happy ending, Rodgers and Hammerstein's *Oklahoma!* is as American as apple pie and broken treaties.

Set in what was then Indian Territory on the cusp of Statehood in the first years of the twentieth

---

* First published in *Counterpunch*, August 18, 2017.

century the beloved musical, which has pulled in endless wagonloads of cash across many Broadway revivals and national tours since its 1943 premiere, makes no mention and offers no glimpse of the non-European inhabitants forcibly put there by Uncle Sam: in *Oklahoma!* the word "Indian" is never spoken nor sung. It's as if the unseen and unheard people whose not-so-distant ancestors had been removed from the Southeast (and elsewhere) after 1830, dying in large numbers on the way, never existed at all. There's a hard-bitten realism to this unreality: The Trail of Tears doesn't put butts in theater seats on Broadway or in Upstate New York.

This erasure is all the more surprising when one recalls that Rodgers and Hammerstein showed themselves adept at ethnic stereotyping in their later musical of 1949, *South Pacific*, in which the Polynesian procuress of a mother, Bloody Mary, casts her exotic spell on American servicemen in her erotic set-piece "Bali Hai"—a tour-de-force of cunning and cliché.

Vast though the American Heartland of *Oklahoma!* may be, there is no space in it for anthropological anthems, however heartless. There are no tom-tom dances nor peace pipe reveries. On the "Beautiful Day" over which most of the musical's action takes place, late in summer when the "corn is as high as an elephant's eye" according to cowboy Curly's hymn to the land that starts the show, no "Braves" or "Squaws" or any colorful Others are to be sighted—excepting, perhaps the furtive, porn addict and hired-hand stalker Jud, who, along with his thwarted desires, probably sports swarthy skin-tones. Needless to say (spoiler alert!), he must be sacrificed at the musical's conclusion so the red-blooded boys can bed their gals and Statehood can come chugging round the corner of the cornfield in the form of a horseless carriage that, in the Glimmerglass production, supplanted the "Surrey with the Fringe on the Top" conjured by Curly in his famous courting chorale.

Jarrett Ott's Glimmerglass Curly was the equivalent of an on-stage rustler: he stole the show right from the get-go, his warm, resonant voice, stubbled granite jaw, and appealing stage manner affecting bluster and self-doubt sent him way ahead of the rest of the cast as soon as the overture was over. Ott was the theatrical equivalent of one of those Boomer Sooners who jumped the starting line for the Native American land grab in the Indian Territory back in 1889. However strong the rest of the show's cast was—and the other youthful players were indeed well-stocked with ability and potential—its members never could quite catch up to Curly's long lines and the vast reach of his baritone ranging all the way to the last row of the opera house. (The building's clever architecture echoes that of a rural barn, though one in a lot better shape than the dozens of dilapidated structures in the post-agrarian Empire State.) Vanessa Becerra's Laurey was both endearing and peppery: the purity of her youthful soprano drew the naiveté from the simplistic hop-along arpeggios and demure scales of "Many A New Day," but also spiced the tune's folksiness and minor inflections with a furtive sexuality.

Each summer season the Glimmerglass Opera festival puts on a classic American musical that abjures the now-customary Broadway practice of miking the performers. The sound of *Oklahoma!* in Cooperstown therefore is much more like the original experience of the 1940s, and it is a rare pleasure to hear a terrific singer such as Ott display his art without the hindrance of amplification. The prevailing convention of sticking microphones to the actors' heads mistakes loudness for accessibility, the result being disorientation and distancing rather than closeness to the character. Also unshackled from this burdensome technology was the orchestra, led with boisterous spirit and finely-tuned precision by conductor James Lowe.

The imaginative stage direction of Molly Smith made clever use of this freedom by having Curly enter from the back of the auditorium for his opening number, his voice rolling out over the audience's heads—a field of white hair that evoked so many corn tassels.

Like all the male characters, Curly is mighty horny—a state that was readily identified with by the sex-starved wartime servicemen of 1943 looking for fun in New York's theater district and nearby Times Square. It was not a time of cultural and racial sensitivity. Japanese internment had been underway for a year. With a grim nod to the Indian Removal Act, two smaller detention relocation centers were set up in Oklahoma for Japanese-Americans. The wide sweeps and endearing steps of Richard Rodgers's melodies only increase the blinding America-for-Americans glare.

Rodgers and Hammerstein were vigilant in their expurgations. They based their musical on Lynn Riggs' 1931 play *How Green Grow the Lilacs*, which includes several lines about the native presence and past, and often refers to the region as Indian Territory, a phrase never uttered in *Oklahoma!* In the second of the play's six scenes, Laurey tells her aged Aunt Eller that "a man found thirty-three arrow heads—thirty-three—whur they'd been a Indian battle." Soon after that the girl asks, "How big is Indian Territory?" and her aunt's reply is meant to be comic: "Oh, big." The implication is that it's big enough for all settlers. But Laurey herself is not settled by the response: "It's a funny place to live, ain't it?" The girl longs for a more refined home where she can be educated and lose the kind of bogus hick diction the playwright has saddled her with. But she's also stating the obvious and painful truth: it's very unfunny to be an invader in someone else's land.

Riggs' play was itself full of songs, even, like *Oklahoma!*, beginning with one about "A bright and sunny morning" sung by the cowpoke hero. One of Riggs' numbers includes a stanza that lays out the racial dynamic that oppresses *Oklahoma!* even though it is scrupulously silenced in the Rodgers and Hammerstein adaptation:

> They rode till they come to the crest of the hill
> Where the Indians shot like hail,
> They poured death's volley on Custer's men,
> And scalped them as they fell.
>
> They turned from the crest of the bloody hills
> With an awful gathering gloom,
> And those that were left of the faithful band
> Rode slowly to their doom.
>
> There was no one left to tell the blue-eyed girl
> The words that her lover said,
> And the praying mother will never know
> That her blue-eyed boy is dead."

The Aryans not the Natives are the tragic victims.

Riggs hailed from Claremore, Oklahoma, the town at the center of the musical, and he boasted a trace of Cherokee blood, drawing autobiographically—and opportunistically—on that ancestry at various points in the play. The wedding night of Curly and Laurey is interrupted by the knife duel-to-the-death with Jud. After slaying his counterpart, the bridegroom is confronted by federal marshals who threaten to take him that very night to the nearest judge. The local folk rally round Curly and resist interference in their affairs: "We hain't furriners. My pappy and mammy was both borned in Indian Territory! Why, I'm jist plumb full of Indian blood myself." Others in the mob are quick to claim their prairie cred: "Me too! And I c'n prove it!" The New Yorkers Rodgers and Hammerstein couldn't say the same: their entertainment didn't have the time for, or interest in race, history, and colonial violence.

In appropriating spurious symbols, from blood to war bonnets, Riggs' sham nativism takes a page right out of the script of one of the earliest of America's homegrown plays—the Boston Tea Party. The Rodgers and Hammerstein whitewashing of Oklahoma for the Great White Way amounts to a literally spectacular colonization of Indian Territory.

It's an ugly, paradoxical patriotism, this robbing of the markers of the displaced and murdered. Not coincidentally, this kind of symbolic violence is visible all over Cooperstown, just as it is all over America. The vintage, manual scoreboard showing the Major League standings near the entrance to the Baseball Hall of Fame has the Atlanta Braves' tomahawk. For the Cleveland Indians there's now a seemingly inoffensive red "C" in place of Chief Wahoo with his big-toothed grin. That egregious mascot appears to have been banished to the dugout (or perhaps pitched into a dugout canoe and shoved off down the Cuyahoga River towards Lake Erie and then, like Chief Joseph before him, to Canada).

A few yards down Main Street from the entrance to the Hall of Fame is a blue-and-gold New York historical marker that informs visitors that "George Croghan, Indian Agent—Land Speculator, lived in a pioneer log house located here 1769-1770." Back then removals and real estate were the national pastime, and Croghan was an all-star. The informative sign then closes the deal: "General James Clinton's Headquarters were located here in 1779." Dispatched to the New York frontier by George Washington to break the morale of the Natives (allied with the British), Clinton burned some forty Iroquois villages. The original inhabitants thus taken care of, America can celebrate its most hallowed sporting rituals on the very ground once dedicated to ethnic cleansing.

On the edge of Cooperstown on the way out of town heading north along the shores of Otsego Lake to Glimmerglass Opera stands the Fenimore Art Museum, where many paintings and heirlooms of the author of the *Last of the Mohicans* can be pondered. The Coopers acquired large swaths of land after the Revolution in and around the town that still bears their name. Scenes from James Fenimore Cooper's Native fiction were a favorite topic of American artists.

Where *Oklahoma!* would later suppress the memory of the Natives its characters displaced,

Cooper had revived them a century before in the red glow of Romanticism. Two large galleries of the museum are devoted to folk art, and include two Cigar Store Indians, the noble savages who neither sing nor smoke.

In the newest section of the museum on a lower level that opens out onto a vast lawn sweeping down to the lake (and past an Iroquois framed house from the 1790s of the type that Clinton burned in large numbers in advance of the Coopers arrival in the area) is the Thaw collection of Native American Art. The holdings include garments and objects made in the Indian Territory. The first to be encountered is a cradle from around 1880 presented to expectant mothers. Though this work of perfect beauty was made out of hide, glass beads, wood, German silver tacks, wool and cotton by an unknown individual woman, it is ascribed simply to the tribe—Kiowa.

The museum curators have marked these items with a boldfaced "O" in reference to the production of *Oklahoma!* being staged a few miles north. The explanatory panel of text projects a message of diversity and hope, not of round-ups, starvation, and death. The same sentiment is also presented in the Glimmerglass opera program book: "Oklahoma was diverse—frontiers always are. African Americans, Native Americans and Asian Americans lived in Oklahoma at the beginning of the twentieth century. They shared a territory, but lived in separate communities. Our production celebrates this diversity, but also reflects modern America, where people from all backgrounds and races live and work together: and the cast reflects this, too."

Thus there are Asian and African and European Americans in the Glimmerglass ensemble, and Aunt Eller is played by the excellent African American actor and singer, Judith Skinner. But this vibrant ethnic tapestry cannot silence the ghosts of *Oklahoma!* At least from the time of African American soprano Leontyne Price's Black Aida at Milan's La Scala in 1960—and before her Marian Anderson—opera audiences have been accustomed to looking past skin color on stage. Now even Verdi's *Otello* can be done without offense-giving blackface.

At Glimmerglass on the Saturday night after *Oklahoma!*, the agile and expressive counter-tenor voice of John Holiday Jr. captivated another sold-out audience in Handel's *Xerxes*. Holiday's skin is of the hue of Miles Davis (photographic portraits of whom are also now on exhibit in the Fenimore Museum's exhibition of Herman Leonard's brilliant images of jazz musicians), and far darker than that of the Persian king he played.

This selective seeing and hearing might help explain why operas and musicals can often insulate themselves from changes in the political weather. Indeed, the continual reprises in *Oklahoma!* of

"Beautiful Morning" and that fetching "Surrey" are an instructive form of built-in nostalgia, recollections not just of the musical itself but of a past that never existed. The Whiteness of *Oklahoma!* yearns not just to forget genocidal crimes but rather to wish them away entirely through its own myth-making song.

Glimmerglass is not so very far from Charlottesville, ethically or geographically. Ignored in the battle over the removal of Robert E. Lee's statue and the racist violence that followed is the fact that before the Civil War the general served as an officer in the U.S. cavalry protecting settlers against the Apache and Comanche in Texas. It is now time to harness that surrey with a fringe on the top to the confederate general's horse, crack the righteous whip and send *Oklahoma!* and the Virginian galloping towards that boundless, borderless Territory of American Amnesia, the motley gig trailing songs in its wake.

Appendix

Dear White American Theater,

We come together as a community of Black, Indigenous, and People of Color (BIPOC) theatremakers, in the legacy of August Wilson's "The Ground on Which I Stand," to let you know exactly what ground we stand on in the wake of our nation's civic unrest.

We see you. We have always seen you. We have watched you pretend not to see us.

We have watched you un-challenge your white privilege, inviting us to traffic in the very racism and patriarchy that festers in our bodies, while we protest against it on your stages. We see you.

We have watched you program play after play, written, directed, cast, choreographed, designed, acted, dramaturged and produced by your rosters of white theatremakers for white audiences, while relegating a token, if any, slot for a BIPOC play. We see you.

We have watched you amplify our voices when we are heralded by the press, but refuse to defend our aesthetic when we are not, allowing our livelihoods to be destroyed by a monolithic and racist critical culture. We see you.

We have watched you inadequately compare us to each other, allowing the failure of entire productions to be attributed to decisions you forced upon us for the comfort of your theater's white patrons. Meanwhile, you continue to deprioritize the broadening of your audiences by building NO relationship with our communities. We see you.

We have watched you harm your BIPOC staff members, asking us to do your emotional labor by writing your Equity, Diversity and Inclusion statements. When we demanded you live up to your own creeds, you cowered behind old racist laments of feeling threatened, and then discarded us along with the values you claim to uphold. We see you.

We have watched you discredit the contributions of BIPOC theatres, only to co-opt and annex our work, our scholars, our talent, and our funding. We see you.

We have watched you turn a blind eye as unions refuse to confront their racism and integrate their ranks, muting the authenticity of our culture and only reserving space for us to shine out front on your stages but never behind them. We see you.

We have watched you dangle opportunities like carrots before emerging BIPOC artists, using the power of development, production, and awards to quiet us into obedience at the expense of our art and integrity. We see you.

We have watched you use our BIPOC faces on your brochures, asking us to politely shuffle at your galas, talkbacks, panels, board meetings, and donor dinners, in rooms full of white faces, without being willing to defend the sanctity of our bodies beyond the stages you make us jump through hoops to be considered for. We see you.

We have watched you hustle for local, federal, foundation and private funding on our backs, only to redirect the funds into general operating accounts to cover your deficits from years of fiscal mismanagement. We see you.

We have watched you hire the first BIPOC artists in executive leadership, only to undermine our innovations and vision of creating equitable institutions, by suffocating our efforts with your fear, inadequacy, and mediocrity. We see you.

We have watched you attend one "undoing racism workshop," espousing to funders you are doing the work, without any changes to your programming or leadership. You've been unwilling to even say the words "anti-racism" to your boards out of fear of them divesting from your institutions, prioritizing their privilege over our safety. We see you.

We have watched you promote anti-Blackness again and again. We see you.

We have watched you say things like–I may be white, but I'm a woman. Or, I may be white, but I'm gay. As if oppression isn't multi-layered. We see you.

We have watched you exploit us, shame us, diminish us, and exclude us. We see you.

We have always seen you.

And now you will see us.

We stand on this ground as BIPOC theatre-makers, multi-generational, at varied stages in our careers, but fiercely in love with the Theatre. Too much to continue it under abuse. We will wrap the least privileged among us in protection, and fearlessly share our many truths.

About theatres, executive leaders, critics, casting directors, agents, unions, commercial producers, universities and training programs. You are all a part of this house of cards built on white fragility and supremacy. And this is a house that will not stand.

This ends TODAY.

We are about to introduce you…to yourself.

Signed,

The Ground We Stand On

About the Contributors

Carla Blank is a writer, director, dramaturge and editor. She co-authored *Storming the Old Boys' Citadel: Two Pioneer Women Architects of Nineteenth Century North America*, with Canadian architectural historian Tania Martin (Baraka Books, 2014). She is author and editor of the 20th century historical reference *Rediscovering America: The Making of Multicultural America, 1900-2000* (Three Rivers Press, 2003) which carries the imprimatur of Before Columbus Foundation. Her two-volume anthology of performing arts techniques and styles, *Live on Stage!* (Dale Seymour Publications, a Pearson Education imprint, 1997, 2000), was co-authored with Jody Roberts. With Ishmael Reed, in addition to this anthology, she co-edited the anthology *Powwow: Charting the Fault Lines in the American Experience, Short Fiction, From Then to Now* (Da Capo Books, 2009). Her essays have appeared in the *San Francisco Chronicle,* the *Wall Street Journal,* the *Buffalo News, Alta, Konch* and *CounterPunch.* A creator of multidisciplinary performance works since childhood, artists she has collaborated with include Suzushi Hanayagi, Robert Wilson, Meredith Monk, Remy Charlip, Sally Gross, Elaine Summers, Genny Lim, Aldo Tambellini, Carman Moore, Ishmael Reed, Wajahat Ali, and Yuri Kageyama. She makes her home in Oakland, California.

Lonely Christopher is the author of the poetry collections *Death & Disaster Series, The Resignation,* and *In a January Would.* He also wrote the short story collection *The Mechanics of Homosexual Intercourse* and the novel *THERE.* His plays have been presented in Canada, China, and the United States. His film credits include several international shorts and the feature *MOM,* which he wrote and directed. He works for homeless queer youth and lives in Brooklyn.

Tommy J. Curry is Personal Chair of Africana Philosophy & Black Male Studies in the Department of Philosophy of The University of Edinburgh, School of Philosophy, Psychology, and Language Sciences. He is Editor of *Black Male Studies: A Series Exploring the Paradoxes of Racially Subjugated Males* (Temple University Press). Dr. Curry has authored *Another white Man's Burden: Josiah Royce Quest for a Philosophy of white Racial Empire* (2018), winner of the Josiah Royce Prize in American Idealist Thought (2020); *The Man-Not: Race, Class, Genre, and the Dilemmas of Black Manhood* (2017), winner of the American Book Award (2018); and *The Philosophical Treatise of William H. Ferris: Selected Readings from The African Abroad or, His Evolution in Western Civilization* (2016).

Jack Foley has published 17 books of poetry, 5 books of criticism, a book of stories, and a 1300-page "chronoencyclopedia," *Visions & Affiliations: California Poetry 1940-2005*. He became well known through his multi-voiced performances with his late wife, Adelle, also a poet. He currently performs with his new life partner, Sangye Land. He has presented poetry on the Pacifica radio station KPFA regularly since 1988 and is currently one of the hosts of KPFA's literary program, *Cover to Cover.*He has received two Lifetime Achievement Awards, one from Marquis *Who's Who* and one from the Berkeley Poetry Festival, and June 5, 2010 was declared "Jack Foley Day" in Berkeley. Two new books of Foley's poetry, *When Sleep Comes: Shillelagh Songs* and *Duet of Polygon*, a collaboration with Japanese poet Maki Starfield, have recently appeared, and poets/ scholars Dana Gioia and Peter Whitfield have published *Jack Foley's Unmanageable Masterpiece*—a book of essays dealing with *Visions & Affiliations*.

Emil Guillermo is an award-winning journalist and commentator, who has worked in TV, radio, and newspapers, from Honolulu to San Francisco to Texas and Washington, D.C., notably as a former host of NPR's *All Things Considered*. Self-described as a "social wittic," he has written his "Emil Amok" column in the ethnic media since 1995, a compilation of which,

Amok: Essays from an Asian American Perspective," won an American Book Award in 2000. His column is now home-based at the Asian American Legal Defense and Education Fund. He has performed his work as a solo theater artist in Fringe Festivals around the country, and at the Filipino American National History Museum, where he is museum director. He is the host of "The PETA Podcasts." His vlog and podcasts are at www.amok. com. Born in San Francisco to a colonized father and immigrant mother from the Philippines, he grew up in the Mission District and graduated from Harvard.

Claire J. Harris is an award-winning writer of fiction, creative non-fiction and screenplays, whose short stories and articles have been published in Australia and internationally. She is also a member of the writers' room for the upcoming Netflix series, *Dive Club,* which is currently in production.

In 2017, Claire released *Zelos,* her debut independent feature film as screenwriter and producer. The film had a well-received run on the international festival circuit, before being screened across six states and territories in Australia. She has two feature screenplays in development with the Steve Jaggi Company, scheduled for production in 2021.

Claire holds a Masters in Writing, and a Graduate Certificate in Screenwriting from the Australian Film Television and Radio School. She is currently based in Melbourne, Australia, where she works as a copywriter and screenwriter. You can find her at www.clairejharris.com.

Yuri Kageyama is a poet, filmmaker and journalist. Her latest book is *The New and Selected Yuri: Writing from Peeling Till Now* (Ishmael Reed Publishing, 2011). She has written and produced two films, *The Very Special Day,* a 2019 collaboration with stop motion artist Hayatto, and *News from Fukushima: Meditation on an Under-Reported Catastrophe by a Poet,* a 2018 Yoshiaki Tago film that documents a performance in San Francisco, directed by Carla Blank. The theater piece brings together Kageyama's poetry and prose with dance, music and video. Her poems and essays are in various literary publications, including *Y'Bird,*

KONCH and *Tokyo Poetry Journal*. She leads her spoken-word band Yuricane. She lives in Tokyo. http://yurikageyama.com/

Soraya Nadia McDonald is the culture critic for *The Undefeated*. She writes about pop culture, fashion, the arts, and literature. She is the 2020 winner of the George Jean Nathan prize for dramatic criticism, a 2020 finalist for the Pulitzer Prize in criticism, and the runner-up for the 2019 Vernon Jarrett Medal.

Nancy Mercado, PhD, was named one of 200 living individuals who best embody the work and spirit of Frederick Douglass, on the bicentennial of his birthday, by the Frederick Douglass Family Initiatives and the Antiracist Research and Policy Center at American University. She is the recipient of the 2017 American Book Award for Lifetime Achievement presented by the Before Columbus Foundation.

Editor of the first Nuyorican Women Writers Anthology published in *Voices e-Magazine* of the Center for Puerto Rican Studies, Hunter College—CUNY, Mercado is a guest curator for the Museum of American Poetics. She has been featured on National Public Radio's *The Talk of the Nation* and on the *PBS NewsHour Special* "America Remembers 9/11" and is the author of *It Concerns the Madness* (a poetry collection), *Las Tres Hermanas* (a children's coloring book), and is the editor of *if the world were mine* (a young adult anthology). Mercado holds a doctoral degree in English Literature. Visit: nancy-mercado.com.

Aimee Phan grew up in Orange County, California, and now teaches writing and literature at California College of the Arts. She is the author of two books of fiction, *The Reeducation of Cherry Truong*, and *We Should Never Meet*, which was named a Notable Book by the Kiryama Prize in fiction and a finalist for the Asian American Literary Awards. She has received fellowships from the NEA, Rockefeller Foundation's Bellagio Center, MacDowell Arts Colony, Headlands Center for the Arts, and Hedgebrook. Her writing has appeared in *The New York Times*, *San Francisco Chronicle*, *USA Today*, and CNN. com, among others.

Ishmael Reed is a poet, novelist, essayist, playwright, song-writer, public media commentator, lecturer and publisher. Author of more than thirty books, *Why the Black Hole Sings the Blues*, his most recent poetry collection, was published in November 2020 by Dalkey Archive Press, which published his eleventh novel, *Conjugating Hindi*, in 2018. Also in 2020, his latest non-fiction work, *Malcolm and Me*, was published by Audible, with Reed as narrator; Audible published Reed's second audio book, a short story, *The Fool Who Thought Too Much*, in November 2020. Baraka Books of Montreal published Reed's latest essay collection, *Why No Confederate Statues in Mexico*, in 2019. New York's Nuyorican Poets Café premiered his ninth and latest produced play, *The Haunting of Lin-Manuel Miranda*, May 23, 2019, which garnered three 2019 AUDELCO awards; the play was published by Archway Editions in October 2020. Reed is founder of the Before Columbus Foundation and PEN Oakland, non-profit organizations run by writers for writers. He is a MacArthur Fellow, and among his other honors are the University of California at Berkeley's Distinguished Emeritus Award for the year 2020, the University of Buffalo's 2014 Distinguished Alumni Award, National Book Award and Pulitzer Prize nominations, and a Lila Wallace-Reader's Digest Award. Awarded the 2008 Blues Songwriter of the Year from the West Coast Blues Hall of Fame, his collaborations with jazz musicians for the past forty years were also recognized by SFJazz Center with his appointment, from 2012-2016, as San Francisco's first Jazz Poet Laureate and in Venice, Italy, where he became the first Alberto Dubito International awardee, honored as "a special artistic individual who has distinguished himself through the most innovative creativity in the musical and lin-guistic languages." Reed's *The Terrible Fours*, the third novel in his *"Terribles"* trilogy, was published by Baraka Books in 2021. A March 2021 virtual reading of Reed's most recent play, *The Slave Who Loved Caviar*, was followed by a full production premiered at Off-Broadway's Theater for the New City in December, 2021. His online international literary magazine, *Konch*, can be found at www.ishmaelreedpub.com. His author website is located at www.ishmaelreed.org.

Betsy Theobald Richards is the Director of Cultural Strategies for the Opportunity Agenda, a social justice communications lab based in New York City. She leads the organization's efforts at the intersection of arts, culture and narrative change. Before joining the Opportunity Agenda, Betsy spent over seven years as a Program Officer in Media, Arts, and Culture at the Ford Foundation overseeing a national portfolio on Native American and place-based arts organizations and cultural communities. Previously, she served as the inaugural Director of Public Programs for the Pequot Museum, the country's largest Native American museum and research center. In addition, she has run two theater companies, served as a Fellow with New York Shakespeare Festival, and directed on stages in New York, Los Angeles and Canada. She is a graduate of New York University and the Yale School of Drama and is a citizen of the Cherokee Nation.

Shawn Wong is the author of two novels, *Homebase* and *American Knees*. He is also the co-editor and editor of six Asian American and American multicultural literary anthologies including the pioneering anthology *Aiiieeeee! An Anthology of Asian American Writers*. *Americanese*, the award-winning film version of *American Knees*, was directed by Eric Byler in 2006. Wong is Professor of English and Cinema & Media Studies at the University of Washington in Seattle. He won the the AUPresses' 2021 Stand UP Award.

David Yearsley has been music critic at "America's Last Newspaper," *The Anderson Valley Advertiser*, since 1990. Author most recently of *Sex, Death, and Minuets: Anna Magdalena Bach and Her Musical Notebooks* (University of Chicago Press, 2019), he writes a column every Friday on music and politics for *CounterPunch*. Professor of music at Cornell University, he has made numerous recordings on historic keyboard instruments—from ancient organs to vintage Moog synthesizers. He has been honored with Humboldt, Wenner-Gren, ACLS and Guggenheim fellowships.

Notes

Foreword: Is Broadway about Dollars and Cents?

1. Teeman, Tom. "See Us, Trust Us, Employ Us: Broadway's Women of Color on Confronting Racism and Reshaping Theater." The Daily Beast updated Aug. 30, 2019. https://www.thedailybeast.com/broadways-women-of-color-on-confronting-racismand-reshaping-theater

2. *Spectrum News* NY1, Oct. 9, 2020. https://www.ny1.com/nyc/all-boroughs/news/2020/10/09/broadway-corona-virus-shutdown-latest-timeline-for-possible-reopening-

3. The Changing Racial and Ethnic Makeup of New York City Neighborhoods, Furman Center for Real Estate and Urban Policy, 2011 https://furmancenter.org/files/sotc/The_Changing_Racial_and_Ethnic_Makeup_of_New_York_City_Neighborhoods_11.pdf

4. Op. cit.

5. *Equity News*. Spring 2017, Data Compiled by Russell Lehrer | Graphics by Nick DeSantis |Special thanks to Doug Beebe, Tom Kaub and Sherry Xu.

6. Ibid.

7. Kennedy, Mark. "Report Finds New York Writers, Stages Remain Extremely White" AP, October 1, 2020.

8. Clement, Olivia. "New AAPAC Report Shows Nearly 90 Percent of Playwrights From 2016–2017 Season White and Mostly Male," *Playbill,* MAR 05, 2019. https://www.playbill.com/article/new-aapac-report-shows-nearly-90-of-play-wrights-from-20162017-season-white-and-mostly-male

9. Teeman, Tom. "See Us, Trust Us, Employ Us: Broadway's Women of Color on Confronting Racism and Reshaping Theater." The Daily Beast updated Aug. 30, 2019. https://www.thedailybeast.com/broadways-women-of-color-on-confronting-racismand-reshaping-theater

10. Teeman, Tom, *Op cit.*

11. DiPaola, Steven. *Actors' Equity 2018-2019 Theatrical Season Report: An Analysis of Employment, Earnings, Membership and Finance.*

12 Sanchez, Hazel. "Tourism Expert Says It Could Take NYC 3 to 5 Years to Recover." CBS2, Nov. 17, 2020. https://newyork.cbslocal.com/2020/11/17/coronavirus-covid-19-new-york-city-tourism/

13. Seymour, Lee. "Why Broadway Is So White, Part 1: Real Estate, Nepotism And David Mamet." *Forbes*, April 7, 2016. https://www.forbes.com/sites/leeseymour/2016/04/07/why-broadway-is-so-white-part-1-real-estate-nepotism-and-david-mamet/#52cd8b1622bb

14. The Broadway League, "The Demographics of the Broadway Audience: 2018-2019 SEASON." Downloaded 10/20/20 from https://www.broadwayleague.com/research/research-reports/

15. Tubbs, Michael. "Broadway Show Ticket Sales Analysis Chart wk 02/23/3030." https://www.nytix.com/news/broadway-show-ticket-sales-analysis-chart-w-e-02-23-2020#:~:text=The%20average%20ticket%20to%20the,which%20is%2060%25%20more%20performances.

16. Ng, David. "Average cost of a Broadway ticket passes $100 for the first time." *The Los Angeles Times,* June 10, 2014. https://www.latimes.com/entertainment/arts/la-et-cm-broadway-ticket-prices-20140610-story.html

17. Cox, Gordon. "Three Dynasties Preside Over Broadway's Theater Houses." *Variety*, October 6, 2017. https://variety.com/2017/legit/features/broadway-theater-dynasties-1202579853/

18. Rubino-Finn, Olivia. "Broadway Budgets 101: Breaking Down the Production Budget" *New Musical Theatre blog*, January 22, 2016. https://newmusicaltheatre.com/blogs/green-room/broadway-budgets-101-breaking-down-the-production-budget

19. Rubino-Finn, Olivia. "Broadway Budgets 101: Breaking Down the Weekly Budget," *New Musical Theatre blog*, Feb. 11,

2016. https://newmusicaltheatre.com/blogs/green-room/broadway-budgets-101-breaking-down-the-weekly-budget-1

20. Ng, David. "Average cost of a Broadway ticket passes $100 for the first time." *The Los Angeles Times*, June 10, 2014. https://www.latimes.com/entertainment/arts/la-et-cm-broadway-ticket-prices-20140610-story.html

21. Seymour, Lee. Op. cit.

22. Marks, Peter. "Read All About It: Why Disney owns the live stage too." *The Washington Post*, Oct. 23, 2019. https://www.washingtonpost.com/entertainment/theater_dance/read-all-about-it-why-disney-owns-the-live-stage-too/2019/10/22/171b56c2-f3ee-11e9-8cf0-4cc99f74d127_story.html https://blog.headout.com/disney-on-broadway/

23. McPhee, Ryan. "Disney Theatrical Productions Reveals Next Steps for *Hercules* and *The Jungle Book* Musicals, *Aida* Revival, More." *Playbill* May 15, 2020. https://www.playbill.com/article/disney-theatrical-productions-reveals-next-steps-for-hercules-and-the-jungle-book-musicals-aida-revival-more

24. Shea, Andrea. "'Porgy and Bess': Messing with a classic." NPR August 20, 2011. https://www.npr.org/2011/08/21/139784251/porgy-and-bess-messing-with-a-classic

25. Dawkins, Sydney-Chanele. "Adapting Porgy and Bess, an Interview with Pulitzer Prize winner Suzan-Lori Parks." DC Metro: Theater Arts, Dec. 26, 2013. https://dcmetrotheaterarts.com/2013/12/26/the-playwrights-playground-part-i-adapting-porgy-and-bess-an-interview-with-pulitzer-prize-winner-suzan-lori-parks-by-sydney-chanele-dawkins/

26. Basler, Derek. "Broadway Crowds Are So White." 2020/01/06. https://blogs.baruch.cuny.edu/dollarsandsense/2020/01/06/broadway-struggles-to-draw-diverse-audiences/

27. Wilson, August. "The Ground on Which I Stand," reprinted by *American Theatre*, June 20, 2016. https://www.americantheatre.org/2016/06/20/the-ground-on-which-i-stand/

28. Clement, Olivia. "300 BIPOC Theatre Artists Call for Reckoning in the White American Theater." *Playbill*, June 09,

2020. https://www.playbill.com/article/300-bipoc-theatre-artists-call-for-reckoning-in-the-white-american-theatre

29. Clement, Olivia. "We See You, White American Theater." *Playbill*, Jan. 13, 2021. https://www.playbill.com/article/bipoc-artists-unveil-demands-for-the-white-american-theatre.

When You Mess with Creation Myths, the Knives Come Out

1. Reed, Ishmael: "'Hamilton' is a bad jingoistic history, but nice eye candy." *Datebook, San Francisco Chronicle*, 27 July 2019.

2. Thomas, Dexter. "Do you hate 'Hamilton'? Now you can see a play about how much it sucks." Article appeared on June 21, 2019, https://www.vice.com/en/article/qv7mab/do-you-hate-hamilton-now-you-can-see-a-play-about-how-much-it-sucks. Program segment on Vice News on HBO (Video).

3. Barrett, William. *The Truants: Adventures Among the Intellectuals*. Anchor Press/Doubleday. New York, 1 January 1982.

4. Wiencek, Henry. *An Imperfect God, George Washington, His Slaves, and the Creation of America*. Farrar, Straus and Giroux. New York, 2003.

5. Prince, Richard. "Uproar Over Race at NPR." *Journalisms*. 7 September 2019. http://www.journal-isms.com/2019/09/uproar-over-race-at-npr/

6. Marcus, Joan, (Kris Virephotography). "The *Hamilton* Exhibition Was Doomed From the Start." *Chicago Mag.* 31 July 2019.

7. Wills, Garry. *"Negro President" Jefferson and the Slave Power*. Houghton Mifflin Harcourt, Boston, New York. 2005.

Also from Baraka Books

FICTION

Exile Blues
Douglas Gary Freeman

Things Worth Burying
Matt Mayr

Fog
Rana Bose

The Daughters'
Murielle Cyr

Yasmeen Haddad Loves Joanasi Maqaittik
Carolyn Marie Souaid

NONFICTION

Journey to the Heart of the First Peoples Collections
Marie-Paule Robitaille

Stolen Motherhood, Surrogacy and Made-to-Order Children
Maria De Koninck

Still Crying for Help, The Failure of Our Mental Healthcare Services
Sadia Messaili

A Distinct Alien Race, The Untold Story of Franco-Americans
David Vermette

The Einstein File, The FBI's Secret War on the World's Most Famous Scientist
Fred Jerome

*Montreal, City of Secrets, Confederate Operations in Montreal
During the American Civil War*
Barry Sheehy

Let's Move On
Paul Okalik with Louis McComber

Patriots, Traitors and Empires, The Story of Korea's Struggle for Freedom
Stephen Gowans

Printed by Imprimerie Gauvin
Gatineau, Québec